Berlitz®

Danish
Phrase Book
and
Dictionary

Contacting the Editors
Every effort has been made to provide accurate information in this publication, but changes are inevitable. The publisher cannot be responsible for any resulting loss, inconvenience or injury. We would appreciate it if readers would call our attention to any errors or outdated information. We also welcome your suggestions; if you come across a relevant expression not in our phrase book, please contact us: Berlitz Publishing, 193 Morris Avenue, Springfield, NJ 07081, USA. Email: comments@berlitzbooks.com

First Printing: May 2008
Printed in Singapore

Publishing Director: Sheryl Olinsky Borg
Senior Editor/Project Manager: Lorraine Sova
Danish Editorial: Sandra Neimann Bird, Christine Thyssen, Annette Morgen
Cover D
Interior
Product
Compos
Cover Pl
Interior I   age fotostock; p. 19 © Danmarks
National Ba   search.com; p. 48 © Purestock/
Alamy; p. 5   hotography/2002-07 Veer
Incorporate   r Larrea/Pixtal/age fotostock; p. 82
© Netfalls/   Alamy; p. 102 © Imageshop.com;
p. 107 © in   Knud Nielsen/2003-2007
Shutterstoc   123 © Stock Connection/2007
Punchstock   © Jupiterimages/Brand X/Corbis;
p. 140 © Stockbyte/Fotosearch.com; p. 142 © Corbis/2006 JupiterImages Corporation; p. 145
© David McKee/2003-2007 Shutterstock, Inc.; p. 147, 155, 164 © 2007 Jupiterimages Corporation;
inside back cover: © H.W.A.C.

Contents

Survival

Food

People

Fun

Special Needs

Resources

Dictionary

Pronunciation

This section is designed to make you familiar with the sounds of Danish by using our simplified phonetic transcription. You'll find the pronunciation of the Danish letters and sounds explained below, together with their "imitated" equivalents. This system is used throughout the phrase book: simply read the pronunciation as if it were English, noting any special rules below.

Stress has been indicated in the phonetic transcription with underlining. Bold on vowels indicates a lengthening of the vowel sound.

Consonants

Letter	Approximate Pronunciation	Symbol	Example	Pronunciation
c	1. before e, i, y, like s in sit	s	**citron**	see·<u>troan</u>
	2. before a, o, u and a consonant, like k in kite	k	**cafeteria**	kah·feh·<u>teh</u>·ree·a
d	1. at the end of the word after a vowel, or between a vowel and unstressed e or i, like th in this[1]	dh	**med**	medh
	2. otherwise, as in English	d	**dale**	<u>da</u>·ler

[1] The letter **d** is not pronounced in **nd** and **ld** at the end of a word or syllable (**guld** = gooll), or before unstressed **e**, **t** or **s** in the same syllable (**plads** = plass).

Letter	Approximate Pronunciation	Symbol	Example	Pronunciation
g	1. at the beginning of a word or syllable, like g in go	g	**glas**	glas
	2. otherwise, like y in yet[2]	y	**sige**	<u>see</u>·yer
hv	like v in view	v	**hvor**	voar
j, hj	like y in yet	y	**ja**	ya
k	1. between vowels, like g in go	g	**ikke**	<u>ig</u>·ger
	2. otherwise like k in kite	k	**kaffe**	<u>kah</u>·fer
ng	like ng in sing	ng	**ingen**	<u>ing</u>·ern
p	1. between vowels, like b in bit	b	**stoppe**	<u>stoh</u>·ber
	2. otherwise like p in pill	p	**pude**	<u>poo</u>·dher
r	at the beginning of a word, pronounced in the back of the throat, but otherwise often omitted	r	**rose**	<u>roa</u>·ser
s	like s in see	s	**skål**	skowl

---

[2] The letter g occasionally sounds like ch in Scottish loch and can sometimes be mute after a, e, o.

Letter	Approximate Pronunciation	Symbol	Example	Pronunciation
sj	usually like sh in sheet	sh	**sjælden**	<u>sheh</u>·lern
t	1. between vowels, like d in do	d	**lytte**	<u>lew</u>·der
	2. otherwise like t in to[3]	t	**torsk**	toarsk

Letters b, f, h, l, m, n, v are generally pronounced as in English.

Vowels

Letter	Approximate Pronunciation	Symbol	Example	Pronunciation
a	1. when long, like a in father	ah	**klare**	<u>klah</u>·rah
	2. when short, like a in cat	a	**hat**	hat
e	1. when long, like er in fern	er	**svare**	<u>svah</u>·rer
	2. when short, like e in met	eh	**let**	leht
i	1. when long, like ee in bee	ee	**ile**	<u>ee</u>·ler
	2. when short, like i in pin	i	**drikke**	<u>drig</u>·ger

---

[3] In nouns that end with an **e**, an **r** is added to create the plural. In verbs that end with an **e**, an **r** at the end indicates the first person form. This **er** sound, in both cases, sounds like **ah**.

Letter	Approximate Pronunciation	Symbol	Example	Pronunciation
o	1. when long, like oa in boat	oa	**sol**	soal
	2. when short, like o in lot	oh	**godt**	goht
u	1. when long, oo in pool	oo	**frue**	fr<u>oo</u>·er
	2. when short, like oa in boat	oa	**luft**	loaft
y	like ew in new	ew	**nyde**	n<u>ew</u>·dher
æ	1. when long, like ay in day	ay	**sæbe**	s<u>ay</u>·ber
	2. when short, like e in get	eh	**ægte**	<u>ehg</u>·ter
ø	like ur in fur	ur	**frøken**	fr<u>ur</u>·kern
å	1. when long, like ow in tow	ow	**åben**	<u>ow</u>·bern
	2. when short, like aw in saw	aw	**sådan**	saw·<u>dan</u>

A vowel is generally long in stressed syllables when it's the final letter or followed by only one consonant. If followed by two or more consonants, or in unstressed syllables, the vowel is generally short.

In or after some vowels, a short puff of air (glottal stop) is added following the sound. The glottal stop significantly changes the meaning of certain words, e.g., **tænder** with a glottal stop means "teeth" whereas **tænder** without a glottal stop means "to turn on". As that foreigners will be understood without using the glottal stop, this sound has not been included in the phonetics.

Sound Combinations

Letter	Approximate Pronunciation	Symbol	Example	Pronunciation
av, af	like ow in now	ow	**hav**	how
ej, eg	like ie in lie	ie	**nej**	nie
ev	like e in get plus oo sound	eu	**levned**	leu·nerdh
ov	like ow in show	ow	**sjov**	show
øj	ike oi in oil	oi	**øje**	oi·er
øv	like o in so	oh	**søvnig**	soh·nee

Dansk (Danish), a North Germanic language related to Norwegian, Swedish and Icelandic, is the official language of Denmark. There are about six million native speakers in Denmark and parts of northern Germany.

Danish is an official language of the autonomous territories of Greenland and the Faroe Islands, in addition to Greenlandic and Faroese.

How to Use This Book

These are the most essential phrases in each section.

Sometimes you see two alternatives in italics, separated by a slash. Choose the one that's right for your situation.

Essential

I'm here on *vacation [holiday]/business*.	**Jeg er her på *ferie/forretningsrejse*.** yie ehr hehr paw *fehr·yer/foh·reht·nings·rie·ser*
I'm going to…	**Jeg skal til…** yie skal til…
I'm staying at the… Hotel.	**Jeg bor på Hotel…** yie boar paw hoa·tehl…

You May See…

TOLD	customs
TOLDFRIE VARER	duty-free goods
VARER AT ANGIVE	goods to declare

At the Hotel

Does the hotel have…? **Har hotellet…?** hah hoa·tehl·erdh…

- a computer
- an elevator [a lift]
- (wireless) internet
- room service

- **en pc** ehn peh seh
- **en elevator** ehn eh·ler·va·toh
- **(trådløst) internet** (trowdh·lurst) in·tah·neht
- **service på værelset** sur·vees paw vehrl·serdh

Words you may see are shown in *You May See* boxes.

Any of the words or phrases preceded by dashes can be plugged into the sentence above.

12

Danish phrases appear in red.

Read the simplified pronunciation as if it were English. For more on pronunciation, see page 7.

Relationships

I'm...   **Jeg er...** yie ehr...

-- single   – **ugift** oo____

-- in a relationship   – **i et ser** ___ursd
                                  foh-hohl

When different gender forms apply, the masculine form is followed by ♂; feminine by ♀.

-- married   – **gift** geel_

-- divorced   – **skilt** skild

I'm widowed.   **Jeg er enkemand**♂**/enke**♀. yie ehr
                                <u>ehn</u>-ker-man♂/<u>ehn</u>-ker♀

▶ For numbers, see page 162.

The arrow indicates a cross reference where you'll find related phrases.

Information boxes contain relevant country, culture and language tips.

i In Denmark, upon meeting, it is customary to shake hands for both men and women. Close friends (male-female/female-female) may give kisses on the cheeks. As a greeting, you could say **Går det godt?** (How's it going?) or **Hva så?** (What's up?). **Hej** (general greeting) in Danish is used both for hello or hi and bye.

You May Hear...

Næste! <u>nehs</u>-der   Next!

Din billet/Dit pas, **tak.** deen <u>bee</u>-lehd/deet   Your *ticket/passport*,
pas tahk   please.

Expressions you may hear are shown in *You May Hear* boxes.

Color-coded side bars identify each section of the book.

13

▼ Survival

Arrival and Departure

Essential

I'm here on *vacation* [holiday]/business.	**Jeg er her på *ferie/forretningsrejse.*** yie ehr hehr paw *fehr·yer/foh·reht·nings·rie·ser*
I'm going to...	**Jeg skal til...** yie skal til...
I'm staying at the...Hotel.	**Jeg bor på Hotel...** yie boar paw hoa·tehl...

You May Hear...

***Din billet/Dit pas**, tak.* deen *bee·*lehd/deet pas tahk	Your *ticket/passport*, please.
Hvad er formålet med din rejse? vadh ehr foh·mow·lehdh medh deen rie·ser	What's the purpose of your visit?
Hvor skal du bo? voar skal doo boa	Where are you staying?
Hvor lang tid skal du være her? voar langh teedh skal doo vay·er hehr	How long are you staying?
Hvem rejser du sammen med? vehm rie·ser doo sahm·ern medh	Who are you with?

Passport Control and Customs ─────

I'm just passing through.	**Jeg er her kun på gennemrejse.** yie ehr hehr koon paw geh·nehm·rie·ser
I would like to declare...	**Jeg vil gerne fortolde...** yie vil gehr·ner for·toh·ler...
I have nothing to declare.	**Jeg har ikke noget at fortolde.** yie hah ig·ger noa·erdh ad foh·toh·ler

Har du noget at fortolde? har doo <u>noa</u>·erdh
ad for·<u>toh</u>·ler

Do you have
anything to declare?

Du skal betale told af det her. doo skal
beh·<u>ta</u>·ler tohl a deh hehr

You must pay duty
on this.

Vær venlig at åbne denne taske. vehr <u>vehn</u>·lee
ad <u>owb</u>·ner <u>deh</u>·ner <u>tas</u>·ger

Please open this
bag.

You May See...

TOLD	customs
TOLDFRIE VARER	duty-free goods
VARER AT ANGIVE	goods to declare
INGEN VARER AT ANGIVE	nothing to declare
TOLDFRIT	duty-free
PASKONTROL	passport control
POLITI	police

Money and Banking

Essential

Where's...?

– the ATM

– the bank

– the currency
exchange office

Hvor er...? voar ehr...

– **pengeautomaten** <u>pehng</u>·er·ow·toa·ma·dern

– **banken** <u>bahnk</u>·ern

– **vekselkontor** <u>vehk</u>·serl·kohn·toar

What time does the bank *open/close*?	**Hvornår *åbner/lukker* banken?** voar·<u>naw</u> <u>owb</u>·nah/<u>loa</u>·gah <u>bahnk</u>·ern
I'd like to change *dollars/pounds* into kroner.	**Jeg vil gerne veksle nogle *dollars/pund* til kroner.** yie vil <u>gehr</u>·ner <u>vehks</u>·ler <u>noa</u>·ler <u>doh</u>·lahs/<u>poon</u> til <u>kroa</u>·ner
I want to cash a traveler's check [cheque].	**Jeg vil gerne indløse en rejsecheck.** yie vil <u>gehr</u>·ner <u>in</u>·lur·ser ehn <u>rie</u>·ser·shehk

ATM, Bank and Currency Exchange ———

Can I exchange foreign currency here?	**Kan jeg veksle penge her?** kan yie <u>vehk</u>·sler <u>pehng</u>·er hehr
What's the exchange rate?	**Hvad er vekselkursen?** vadh ehr <u>vehk</u>·serl·koor·sern
How much is the fee?	**Hvor meget beregner du i kommission?** voar <u>mie</u>·erdh beh·<u>rie</u>·ner doo ee koa·mee·<u>shoan</u>
I've lost my traveler's checks [cheques].	**Jeg har tabt mine rejsechecks.** yie hah tahbd <u>mee</u>·ner <u>rie</u>·ser·shehks
My card was lost.	**Jeg har tabt mit kort.** yie hah tahbd meed kawd
My credit cards were stolen.	**Mine kort er blevet stjålet.** <u>mee</u>·ner kawd ehr <u>bleh</u>·verdh <u>stjow</u>·lerd
My card doesn't work.	**Mit kort virker ikke.** meed kawd <u>veer</u>·gah <u>ig</u>·ger

▶ For numbers, see page 162.

You May See…

INDSÆT DIT KORT	insert card
ANNULLER	cancel
SLET	clear
INDTAST	enter
PINKODE	PIN
UDBETALING	withdraw funds
FRA DIN CHECKKONTO	from checking [current account]
FRA DIN OPSPARINGSKONTO	from savings
KVITTERING	receipt

Cash can be obtained from **pengeautomater** (ATMs), which are located throughout Denmark. Some debit cards (with the Plus and Cirrus logos) and most major credit cards are accepted. Be sure you know your PIN and whether it is compatible with European machines, which usually expect a four-digit, numeric code. ATMs offer good rates, though there may be some hidden fees.

Vekselkontor (currency exchange offices) and **banker** (banks) are options for exchanging currency. Exchange offices are found in many tourist centers. Banks in Copenhagen are open Monday to Friday 9:30 a.m. to 4 p.m., though some close later on Thursday. Currency exchange offices and banks charge similar fees to exchange money. Remember to bring your passport, in case you are asked for identification.

You May See…

Denmark, Norway and Sweden all use the same name for their currency, but the value differs in each country. The **krone** (meaning "crown", pronounced <u>kroa</u>·ner and abbreviated **kr.** or **DKK**), is divided into 100 **øre** (pronounced <u>ur</u>·er).

Coins: 25 and 50 **øre**, 1, 2, 5, 10 and 20 **kroner**

Notes: 50, 100, 200, 500 and 1,000 **kroner**

Transportation

Essential

How do I get to town?	**Hvordan kommer jeg ind til byen?** voar·dan kohm·ah yie in til bew·ern
Where's...?	**Hvor er...?** voar ehr...
– the airport	– **lufthavnen** loaft·hown·ern
– the train [railway] station	– **togstationen** tow·sta·shoa·nern
– the bus station	– **busstationen** boos·sta·shoa·nern
– the subway [underground] station	– **metrostationen** meh·troa·sta·shoan·nern
How far is it?	**Hvor langt er der?** voar lahngt ehr dehr
Where can I buy tickets?	**Hvor køber man billetter?** voar kur·ber man bee·leh·dah
A *one-way [single]/round-trip [return]* ticket.	**En *enkeltbillet/returbillet.*** ehn ehn·kerld·bee·lehd/reh·toor·bee·lehd
How much?	**Hvor meget koster det*?** voar mie·erdh kohs·dah deh
Are there any discounts?	**Er der nogen rabatter?** ehr der noa·ern rah·ba·dah
Which...?	**Hvilken...?** vil·kern...
– gate	– **gate** gayd
– line	– **tog** tow
– platform	– **perron** peh·rohng

---

* For information on **det** and **den**, see page 161.

Where can I get a taxi?	**Hvor kan jeg få en taxa?** voar kan yie fow ehn <u>tahk</u>·sa	
Take me to this address.	**Kør mig til denne adresse.** kur mie til <u>deh</u>·ner a·<u>drah</u>·ser	
Where can I rent a car?	**Hvor kan jeg leje en bil?** voar kan yie <u>lie</u>·er ehn beel	
Can I have a map?	**Har du et vejkort?** har doo eht <u>vie</u>·kawd	

Ticketing

When's…to Århus?	**Hvornår afgår…til Århus?** voar·<u>naw</u> ow·gaw…til **<u>aw</u>**·hoos
– the first bus	– **den første bus** dehn <u>fur</u>·sder boos
– the next flight	– **det næste fly** deh <u>nehs</u>·der flew
– the last train	– **det sidste tog** deh <u>sees</u>·der tow
Where can I buy tickets?	**Hvor køber man billetter?** voar <u>kur</u>·ber man bee·<u>lehd</u>·ah
One ticket/Two tickets, please.	**En billet/To billetter, tak.** ehn bee·<u>lehd</u>/toa bee·<u>leh</u>·dah tahk
For *today/tomorrow*.	**Til *i dag/i morgen*.** til ee·<u>dah</u>/ee·<u>mawn</u>

▶ For days, see page 165.

▶ For time, see page 164.

…ticket.	**…billet.** …bee·<u>lehd</u>
– A one-way [single]	– **En enkelt** ehn <u>ehn</u>·kerld
– A round-trip [return]	– **En retur** ehn reh·<u>toor</u>
– A first class	– **En førsteklasse** ehn <u>furs</u>·der <u>kla</u>·ser
– An economy class	– **En økonomiklasse** ehn ur·koa·noa·<u>mee</u>·kla·ser
How much?	**Hvor meget?** voar <u>mie</u>·erdh

Is there a discount for...?	**Er der rabat for...?** ehr dehr rah·bat foh...
– children	**– børn** burn
– students	**– studerende** stoo·deh·reh·ner
– senior citizens	**– pensionister** pang·shoa·nees·dah
I have an e-ticket.	**Jeg har en e-billet.** yie har ehn eh·bee·lehd
Can I buy a ticket on the bus/train?	**Kan jeg købe en billet i *bussen/toget*?** kan yie kur·ber ehn bee·lehd ee *boo·sern/tow·erdh*
I'd like to...my reservation.	**Jeg vil gerne...min bestilling.** yie vil gehr·ner...meen beh·stil·ing
– cancel	**– annullere** a·noo·leh·rah
– change	**– ændre** ehn·drer
– confirm	**– bekræfte** beh·krehf·der

Plane

Getting to the Airport

How much is a taxi to the airport?	**Hvor meget koster en taxa til lufthavnen?** voar mie·erdh kohs·dah ehn tahk·sa til loaft·how·nern
I would like to go to...Airport, please.	**Jeg vil gerne til...Lufthavn, tak.** yie vil gehr·ner til...loaft·hown tahk
My airline is...	**Jeg skal flyve med...** yie skal flew·er medh...
My flight leaves at...	**Mit fly afgår klokken...** meet flew ow·gaw kloh·gehrn...

▶ For time, see page 164.

I'm in a rush.	**Jeg har travlt.** yie har trowlt
Can you take an alternate route?	**Kan du køre ad en anden rute?** kan doo kur·rah adh ehn a·nern roo·ter
Can you drive *faster/slower*?	**Kan du køre *hurtigere/langsommere*?** kan doo kur·er *hoor·dee·ah/lang·sohm·ah*

You May Hear…

Hvilket flyselskab rejser du med? <u>vil</u>·gerdh <u>flew</u>·sehl·skab <u>rie</u>·ser doo medh — What airline are you flying?

Indenrigs eller udenrigs? in·ern·<u>rees</u> ehl·er <u>oo</u>·dhern·rees — Domestic or International?

Hvilken terminal? <u>vil</u>·gern tehr·mee·<u>nal</u> — What terminal?

You May See…

ANKOMST	arrivals
AFGANG	departures
AFGANGSGATES	departure gates
CHECK-IN SKRANKE	check-in desk
E-BILLET CHECK-IN	e-ticket check-in
BAGAGEBÅND	baggage claim
INDENRIGSFLY	domestic flights
UDENRIGSFLY	international flights

Check-in and Boarding

Where is the check-in desk for flight…? — **Hvor er check-in skranken for fly…?** voar ehr chek·<u>in</u> <u>skrahng</u>·gern foh flew…

My name is… — **Mit navn er…** meet nown ehr…

I'm going to… — **Jeg skal til…** yie skal til…

How much luggage is allowed? — **Hvor meget baggage må jeg have med?** voar <u>mie</u>·erdh ba·<u>ga</u>·sher mow yie ha medh

Which gate does flight…leave from? — **Hvilken gate afgår fly…fra?** <u>vil</u>·gern gayd <u>ow</u>·gaw flew…frah

I'd like *a window/an aisle* seat.	**Jeg vil gerne bede om et *vinduessæde/ sæde ved midtergangen*.** yie vil gehr·ner beh ohm ehd *vin·doos·say·dher/say·dher vedh mi·dah·gahng·ern*
When do we *leave/ arrive*?	**Hvornår *flyver/ankommer* vi?** voar·naw *flew·ah/an·kohm·ah* vee
Is there any delay on flight…?	**Er fly…forsinket?** ehr flew…foh·sing·kerdh
How late will it be?	**Hvor forsinket er det?** voar foh·sing·kerdh ehr deh

Næste! nehs·der	Next!
***Din billet/Dit pas*, tak.** deen *bee·lehd/deet pas* tahk	Your *ticket/passport*, please.
Hvor mange stykker baggage har du? voar mahng·er sdur·ger ba·ga·sher hah doo	How many pieces of luggage do you have?
Du har for meget baggage med. doo hah foh mie·erdh ba·ga·sher mehdh	You have excess baggage.
Den er for *tung/stor* som håndbagage. dehn ehr foh *toang/stoar* som hawn·ba·ga·sher	That's too *heavy/ large* for a carry-on [to carry on board].
Har du selv pakket dine tasker? hah doo sehl pah·kehrd dee·ner tas·ger	Did you pack these bags yourself?
Har nogen bedt dig om at tage noget med? hah noa·ern behd die ohm ad ta noa·erdh mehdh	Did anyone give you anything to carry?
Tøm dine lommer. turm dee·ner loh·mah	Empty your pockets.
Tag dine sko af. ta dee·ner skoa a	Take off your shoes.
Nu begynder vi at boarde fly… noo beh·gur·nah vee ad boar·der flew…	Now boarding flight…

Luggage

Where *is/are*...?	**Hvor er...?** voar ehr...
– the luggage carts [trolleys]	– **bagagevognene** ba·<u>ga</u>·sher·vow·nehr·ner
– the luggage lockers	– **bagageboksene** ba·<u>ga</u>·sher·bohk·ser·ner
– the baggage claim	– **bagagebåndene** ba·<u>ga</u>·sher·bawn·er·ner

My luggage has been lost. **Min bagage er gået tabt.** meen ba·<u>ga</u>·sher erh <u>gow</u>·erdh tahbt

My luggage has been stolen. **Min bagage er blevet stjålet.** meen ba·<u>ga</u>·sher erh <u>bleh</u>·verdh st<u>jow</u>·lerdh

My suitcase was damaged. **Min kuffert er blevet beskadiget.** meen <u>koa</u>·fahd erh <u>bleh</u>·verdh beh·<u>ska</u>·dhee·erd

Finding Your Way

Where is...?	**Hvor er...?** voar ehr...
– the currency exchange office	– **vekselkontoret** <u>vehk</u>·serl·kohn·<u>toar</u>·erd
– the car rental [hire]	– **biludlejningen** <u>beel</u>·oodh·lie·ning·ern
– the exit	– **udgangen** <u>oodh</u>·gahng·ern
– the taxi stand [rank]	– **taxaholdupladsen** <u>tahk</u>·sa·hohl·er·pla·sern
– the subway [underground]	– **metroen** <u>meh</u>·troa·**ern**

Is there a *bus/train* into town? **Kører der *en bus/et tog* ind til byen?** <u>kur</u>·rah dehr *ehn boos/eht tow* in til <u>bew</u>·ern

▶ For directions, see page 34.

Train

How do I get to the train station? **Hvordan kommer jeg hen til togstationen?** voar·<u>dan</u> <u>kom</u>·er yie hehn til tow·sta·sh<u>oa</u>·nern

Is it far? **Er det langt herfra?** ehr deh lahngd hehr·<u>frah</u>

Where *is/are*...?	**Hvor er...?** voar ehr...
– the ticket office	– **billetlugen** bee·<u>lehd</u>·loo·ern
– the information desk	– **informationslugen** in·foh·ma·<u>shoa</u>ns·loo·ern
– the luggage lockers	– **bagageboksene** ba·<u>ga</u>·sher·bohk·ser·ner
– the platforms	– **perronerne** pehr·<u>rohng</u>·ah·ner

▶For directions, see page 34.

▶For ticketing, see page 21.

You May See...

TIL PERRONERNE	to the platforms
INFORMATION	information
PLADSRESERVERINGEN	reservations
ANKOMST	arrivals
AFGANG	departures

Questions

I'd like a schedule [timetable].	**Jeg vil gerne bede om en køreplan.** yie vil <u>gehr</u>·ner beh ohm ehn <u>kur</u>·ah·plan
How long is the trip [journey]?	**Hvor længe tager turen?** voar <u>layng</u>·er t<u>ah</u> <u>too</u>·rern
Do I have to change trains?	**Skal jeg skifte tog?** skal yie <u>skeef</u>·der tow

The Danish train network connects towns across the main islands and the Jutland peninsula. Which train you choose depends on your destination and how quickly you want to get there. **S-bane** or **S-tog** is a commuter train, which serves Copenhagen and surrounding areas. Regional trains and **InterCity** (express) trains travel between Copenhagen and other parts of the country. The **Øresund** train connects Copenhagen and Malmö, Sweden.

A number of discounts are offered depending on the traveler (students, senior citizens, groups, families and children receive considerable reductions), day and time of travel (off-peak times are more highly discounted) as well as the destination. S-trains, the subway and buses run on an integrated network, so you may transfer without paying any additional cost. Keep in mind that buying a **rabatkort** (10-trip ticket), valid for a specified number of zones, is cheaper than buying single tickets. You may also want to consider a 24-hour or 72-hour **CPHCARD** (Copenhagen Card), which offers unlimited train, bus and subway transportation, free entry to over 60 museums and attractions and other discounts. The **CPHCARD** can be purchased online, at tourist offices, in the airport and at major train stations.

Departures

Which platform does the train to…leave from?	**Fra hvilket spor afgår toget til…?** frah vil·kerdh spoar <u>ow</u>·gaw <u>tow</u>·erdh til…

Is this the track [platform] to...?	**Er det her den rigtige perron til...?** ehr deh hehr dehn <u>rig</u>·tee·er pehr·<u>rohng</u> til...
Where is track [platform]...?	**Hvor er perron nummer...?** voar ehr pehr·<u>rohng</u> <u>noa</u>·mah...
Where do I change for...?	**Hvor skal jeg skifte tog til...?** voar ska yie <u>skeef</u>·der tow til...

Boarding

| Is this seat taken? | **Er denne siddeplads optaget?** ehr <u>dehn</u>·er si·dher·plas <u>op</u>·ta·erdh |
| I think that's my seat. | **Det er vist min siddeplads.** deh ehr vist meen si·dher·plas |

You May Hear...

Alle i toget! <u>a</u>·ler ee <u>tow</u>·erdh	All aboard!
Billetter, tak. bee·<u>lehd</u>·ah tahk	Tickets, please.
Du skal skifte i... doo skal <u>skeef</u>·der ee...	You have to change at...
Næste stop er... <u>neehs</u>·der stohp ehr...	Next stop...

Bus

Where's the bus station?	**Hvor ligger busstationen?** voar <u>li</u>·gah boos·sta·shoa·nern
How far is it?	**Hvor langt er der?** voar langt ehr dehr
How do I get to...?	**Hvordan kommer jeg til...?** voar·<u>dan</u> <u>koh</u>·mah yie til...
Does the bus stop at...?	**Stopper bussen ved...?** <u>stoh</u>·bah <u>boo</u>·sern vedh...
Can you tell me when to get off?	**Vil du sige til, når jeg skal af?** vil doo <u>see</u>·yer til naw yie skal a

Do I have to change buses?	**Er det nødvendigt at skifte bus?** ehr deh nurdh-<u>vehn</u>-deed ad <u>skeef</u>-der boos
Stop here, please!	**Jeg skal af her!** yie skal a hehr

▶ For ticketing, see page 21.

Danish buses often continue travel where train lines end. Combining bus and train travel is very easy. You'll find that many bus stations are located next to train stations, their arrival and departure schedules are closely timed and you can use your train ticket to continue your trip on the bus or vice versa. Taking the bus or combining train and bus travel is in fact often faster than train-only travel since many bus connections are more direct than train connections.

You May See...

BUSSTOP	bus stop
INDGANG/UDGANG	enter/exit
DU SKAL STEMPLE DIN BILLET	stamp your ticket

Subway [Underground]

Where's the nearest subway [underground] station?	**Hvor er den nærmeste metrostation?** voar ehr dehn <u>nehr</u>-meh-ster <u>meh</u>-troa-sta-shoan
Which line for...?	**Hvilket tog skal jeg tage til...?** <u>vil</u>-kerdh tow skal yie ta til...
Where do I change for...?	**Hvor skal jeg skifte til...?** voar skal yie <u>skeef</u>-der til...
Is this the right train for...?	**Kører det her tog til...?** <u>kur</u>-rah deh hehr tow til...
Where are we?	**Hvor er vi henne?** voar ehr vee <u>heh</u>-ner

▶ For ticketing, see page 21.

Copenhagen's **Metro** (subway) is a clean, quick and convenient way to travel through the city. You can purchase a **rabatkort** (10-trip ticket) or a 24-hour or 72-hour **CPHCARD** (Copenhagen Card) for discounted fares. Tickets for the **Metro** are interchangeable with those for buses and trains. Tickets must be stamped on the platform before boarding. Note that traveling without a valid ticket may lead to a sizeable fine.

Boat and Ferry

When is the next boat to...?	**Hvornår går den næste båd til...?** voar·<u>naw</u> gaw dehn <u>nes</u>·der bowdh til...
Can I take my car?	**Må jeg tage min bil med?** mow yie ta meen beel medh

▶ For ticketing, see page 21.

You May See...

REDNINGSBÅD	life boats
REDNINGSVEST	life jackets

Denmark is comprised of some 500 islands. Though most of the larger islands are linked by bridges, ferries are a way of life in Denmark. There is regular local as well as international ferry service from Denmark to the Baltic States, England, Germany, Norway, Poland and Sweden. Passenger and car reservations can be made in advance via any travel agency.

Bicycle and Motorcycle

I'd like to rent...	**Jeg vil gerne leje...** yie vil <u>gehr</u>·ner <u>lie</u>·er...
– a bicycle	**– en cykel** ehn <u>sew</u>·gerl
– a moped	**– en knallert** ehn <u>kna</u>·lahd

– a motorcycle	**– en motorcykel** ehn <u>moa</u>·tah·sew·gerl
How much per *day/week*?	**Hvad koster det per *dag/uge*?** vadh <u>kohs</u>·dah deh pehr da/<u>oo</u>·er
Can I have a *helmet/lock*?	**Kan jeg få en *hjelm/lås*?** kan yie fow ehn yehlm/lows

---

Cycling is very much a part of daily life in Denmark and a regular means of transportation for many Danes. Great investment has been made in recent years to keep Copenhagen bike-friendly, prompting it to be labeled the "City of Cyclists" of late. Bikes may be borrowed, free of charge, at one of the approximately 125 City Bike Parking spots around the city. All you have to do is leave a deposit that is returned to you when you bring the bike back to any City Bike Parking rack.

Taxi

Where can I get a taxi?	**Hvor kan jeg få en taxa?** voar kan yie fow ehn <u>tahk</u>·sa
I'd like a taxi *now/for tomorrow* at…	**Jeg vil gerne bestille en taxa *nu/til i morgen* klokken…** yie vil <u>gehr</u>·ner beh·<u>sti</u>·ler ehn <u>tahk</u>·sa noo/til ee <u>moh</u>·wern <u>kloh</u>·gehrn…
Pick me up at (*place/time*)…	**Hent mig *på/klokken*…** hehnt mie paw/<u>kloh</u>·gehrn…
Please take me to…	**Kør mig til…** kur mie til…
– this address	**– denne adresse** <u>deh</u>·ner a·<u>drah</u>·ser
– the airport	**– lufthavnen** <u>loaft</u>·how·nern
– the train station	**– togstationen** tow·sta·sh<u>oa</u>·nern
I'm in a hurry.	**Jeg har travlt.** yie hah trowlt
Can you drive *faster/slower*?	**Kan du køre *hurtigere/langsommere*?** kan doo <u>kur</u>·ah <u>hoor</u>·dee·ah/<u>lang</u>·sohm·ah

Stop/Wait here.	*Stands/Vent* her. *stans/vehnd* hehr
How much?	**Hvor meget koster det?** voar <u>mie</u>·erdh <u>kohs</u>·dah deh
You said…kroner.	**Du sagde…kroner.** doo <u>sa</u>·er…<u>kroa</u>·nah
Keep the change.	**Behold byttepengene.** beh·<u>hohl</u> <u>bew</u>·der·pehng·ah·ner

i Taxis can be hailed in the street. Just look for the **FRI** (free) sign. Taxis can also be found at taxi stands at airports and train stations or ordered by phone. All cabs are metered and service charges are included in the fare, so tipping is not necessary. Most taxis accept credit cards; however, if you're not carrying cash, be sure to check first.

Car

Car Rental [Hire]

Where can I rent a car?	**Hvor kan jeg leje en bil?** voar kan yie <u>lie</u>·er ehn beel
I'd like to rent…	**Jeg vil gerne leje…** yie vil <u>gehr</u>·ner <u>lie</u>·er…
– a *2-door/4-door* car	– **en *to-dørs/fire-dørs* bil** ehn *toa·durs/ feer·durs* beel
– an automatic	– **en bil med automatgear** ehn beel mehdh ow·toa·<u>mad</u> geer
– a car with air conditioning	– **en bil med klimaanlæg** ehn beel medh <u>klee</u>·ma·<u>an</u>·<u>lay</u>g
– a car seat	– **et barnesæde** eht <u>bah</u>·ner·<u>say</u>·dher

How much is it...?	**Hvor meget koster det...?** voar **mie**·erdh kohs·dah deh...
– per *day/week*	– **per *dag/uge*** pehr *da/**oo**·er*
– per kilometer	– **per kilometer** pehr kee·loa·**meh**·dah
– for unlimited mileage	– **med ubegrænset kørsel** medh **oo**·beh·grehn·serdh kur·sehl
– with insurance	– **med forsikring** medh foh·**sik**·ring

You May Hear...

Har du et internationalt kørekort? har doo et in·tah·na·shoa·nalt kur·rah·kawd	Do you have an international driver's license?
Må jeg se dit pas? mow yie seh deet pas	May I see your passport?
Ønsker du at tegne forsikring? urn·sgah doo ad tie·ner for·sik·ring	Do you want insurance?
Du skal betale et depositum på... doo skal beh·ta·ler eht deh·poa·see·toam paw...	There's a deposit of...
Underskriv venligst her. oa·nah·sgreev vehn·leesd hehr	Sign here.

Gas [Petrol] Station

Where's the nearest gas [petrol] station?	**Hvor er den nærmeste benzinstation?** voar ehr dehn nehr·mer·ster behn·seen·sta·shoan
Fill it up, please.	**Fuld tank, tak.** fool tahnk tahk
...liters, please.	**...liter benzin.** ...lee·dah behn·seen
I'd like to pay *in cash/ by credit card*.	**Jeg vil gerne betale *kontant/med kreditkort*.** yie vil gehr·ner beh·ta·ler *kohn·tant/mehdh kreh·deet·kawd*

You May See...

95 OKTAN	regular
98 OKTAN	super
DIESEL	diesel

Asking Directions

Are we on the right road for...?	**Er det den rette vej til...?** ehr deh dehn <u>reh</u>·der vie til...
How far is it to...?	**Hvor langt er der til...?** voar lahngt ehr dehr til...
Where's...?	**Hvor er...?** voar ehr...
– ...Street	– **...gade** ...<u>ga</u>·dher
– this address	– **denne adresse** <u>deh</u>·ner ah·<u>drah</u>·ser
– the highway [motorway]	– **motorvejen** <u>moa</u>·tah·vie·ern
Can you show me on the map?	**Kan du vise mig det på kortet?** kan doo <u>vee</u>·ser mie deh paw <u>kaw</u>·derdh
I'm lost.	**Jeg er faret vild.** yie ehr <u>fah</u>·erdh veel

You May Hear...

ligeud <u>lee</u>·er·oodh	straight ahead
til venstre til <u>vehn</u>·sdrah	on the left
til højre til <u>hoi</u>·ah	on the right
på/rundt om hjørnet *paw/roundt ohm* <u>yu</u>r·nerdh	*on/around* the corner
overfor... <u>ow</u>·ah·foh...	opposite...
bagved... <u>ba</u>·vehdh...	behind...
ved siden af... vehdh <u>see</u>·dhern a...	next to...
efter... <u>ehf</u>·dah...	after...

nord/syd noar/sewdh	north/south
øst/vest ursd/vehsd	east/west
ved trafiklyset vedh trah·<u>feeg</u>·lew·serdh	at the traffic light
ved vejkrydset vedh <u>vie</u>·krew·serdh	at the intersection

Parking

Can I park here?	**Må jeg parkere her?** mow yie pah·<u>keh</u>·ah hehr
Is there a parking lot [car park] nearby?	**Er der en parkeringsplads i nærheden?** ehr dehr ehn pah·<u>keh</u>·rings·plas ee <u>nehr</u>·heh·dhern
How much is it...?	**Hvor meget koster det...?** voar <u>mie</u>·erdh <u>kohs</u>·dah deh...
– per hour	**– per time** pehr <u>tee</u>·mer
– per day	**– per dag** pehr da
– overnight	**– for natten** foh <u>na</u>·dern

Parking in Denmark is restricted. Metered zones allow up to three hours of parking. In Copenhagen, in unmetered zones, there are ticket vending machines where you can pay with coins and bills or by credit card. The ticket should be in a visible place on the dashboard of your car.

Breakdown and Repairs

My car *broke down/ won't start.*	**Min bil** *har fået motorstop/vil ikke* **starte.** meen beel har <u>fow</u>·erdh <u>moa</u>·tah·stohb/ vil <u>ig</u>·ger <u>stah</u>·der
Can you fix it?	**Kan du reparere den?** kan doo reh·pah·<u>rehr</u> dehn
When will it be ready?	**Hvornår er den klar?** voar·<u>naw</u> ehr dehn klah
How much?	**Hvor meget koster det?** voar <u>mie</u>·erdh <u>kohs</u>·dah deh

Accidents

There's been an accident.	**Der er sket en ulykke.** dehr ehr skeht ehn <u>oo</u>·lew·ger
Call *an ambulance/ the police.*	**Ring hurtigt efter *en ambulance/ politiet.*** ring <u>hoor</u>·deet <u>ehf</u>·dah *ehn ahm·boo·<u>lahng</u>·ser/poa·lee·<u>tee</u>·erdh*

Accommodations

Essential

Can you recommend a hotel?	**Kan du anbefale et hotel?** kan doo <u>an</u>·beh·fa·ler eht hoa·<u>tehl</u>
I have a reservation.	**Jeg har bestilt værelse.** yie har beh·<u>stild</u> <u>vehrl</u>·ser
My name is…	**Mit navn er…** meet nown ehr…
Do you have a room…?	**Har I et værelse…?** har ee ehd <u>vehrl</u>·ser…
– for *one/two*	– **enkeltværelse/dobbeltværelse** <u>ehn</u>·kerld·<u>vehrl</u>·ser/<u>doh</u>·berld·<u>vehrl</u>·ser
– with a bathroom	– **med bad** mehdh badh
– with air conditioning	– **med klimaanlæg** mehdh <u>klee</u>·ma·an·layg
– for tonight	– **for i nat** for ee nad
– for two nights	– **for to nætter** for toa <u>nay</u>·dah
– for one week	– **for en uge** for ehn <u>oo</u>·er
How much?	**Hvor meget koster det?** voar <u>mie</u>·erdh <u>kohs</u>·dah deh
Do you have anything cheaper?	**Har du noget billigere?** har doo <u>noa</u>·erdh <u>bee</u>·leer

When's check-out?	**Hvornår skal vi tjekke ud?** voar·<u>naw</u> skal vee <u>tjeh</u>·ker oodh
Can I leave this in the safe?	**Må jeg lade dette være i boksen?** mow yie la <u>deh</u>·ter <u>vay</u>·er i <u>bohk</u>·sern
Can I leave my bags?	**Må jeg lade mine tasker være her?** mow yie la m<u>ee</u>·ner <u>tas</u>·gah <u>vay</u>·ah hehr
Can I have *the bill/ a receipt*?	**Kan jeg få *regningen/en kvittering*?** kan yie fow <u>*rie*</u>·ning·ern/ehn kvee·<u>teh</u>·ring
I'll pay *in cash/by credit card*.	**Jeg vil gerne betale *kontant/med kreditkort*.** yie vil <u>gehr</u>·ner beh·<u>ta</u>·ler *kohn·<u>tahnt</u>/mehdh kreh·<u>deet</u>·kawd*

Finding Lodging

Can you recommend a hotel?	**Kan du anbefale et hotel?** kan doo <u>an</u>·beh·<u>fa</u>·ler eht hoa·<u>tehl</u>
What is it near?	**Hvad ligger det i nærheden af?** vadh <u>li</u>·gah deh ee <u>nehr</u>·heh·dhern a
How do I get there?	**Hvordan kommer jeg derhen?** voar·<u>dan</u> <u>koh</u>·mer yie dehr·<u>hehn</u>

In Denmark, there is a variety of accommodation options in addition to hotels, which range from one to five stars. You could choose to stay in a bed and breakfast, such as a **kro** (country inn), in an old **slot** (castle) or a **motel** (motel). If you are traveling by car, good options include **vandrerhjem** (a hostel), **ungdomsherberg** (a student hotel) or **sommerhus** (a summer house), which refers to any rented living space, such as a seaside cottage or apartment. For a unique vacation experience, you might choose a **bondegårdsferie** (farmhouse stay), which lets you taste Danish farm life firsthand.

Advanced reservations are recommended particularly during the high season. If you arrive in Denmark without a reservation, tourist information offices can assist in locating accommodations as can the Room Reservation Service, found at Central Train Station in Copenhagen.

At the Hotel

I have a reservation.	**Jeg har en reservation.** yie h**ah** ehn reh·sah·va·<u>shoan</u>
My name is…	**Mit navn er…** meet nown ehr…
Do you have a room…?	**Har I et ledigt værelse…?** hah ee edh <u>leh</u>·dheed v**eh**rl·ser…
– with a bathroom	– **med bad** mehdh badh
– with air conditioning	– **med klimaanlæg** mehdh <u>klee</u>·ma·an·layg
– that's *smoking/ non-smoking*	– **ryger/ikke-ryger** <u>rew</u>·ah/<u>ig</u>·ger <u>rew</u>·ah
– for tonight	– **for i nat** foh ee nad
– for two nights	– **for to nætter** foh toa <u>nay</u>·dah
– for one week	– **for en uge** foh ehn <u>oo</u>·er

▶ For numbers, see page 162.

Does the hotel have…?	**Har hotellet…?** hah hoa·<u>tehl</u>·erdh…
– a computer	– **en pc** ehn peh <u>seh</u>
– an elevator [a lift]	– **en elevator** ehn eh·ler·<u>va</u>·toh
– (wireless) internet	– **(trådløst) internet** (<u>trowdh</u>·lurst) in·tah·neht
– room service	– **service på værelset** <u>sur</u>·vees paw <u>vehrl</u>·serdh
– a gym	– **et motionscenter** ehd moa·<u>shoan</u>·sehn·dah
I need…	**Jeg skal bruge…** yie skal broo·er…
– an extra bed	– **en ekstra seng** ehn <u>ehk</u>·strah sehng
– a cot	– **en klapseng** ehn <u>klahp</u>·sehng
– a crib [child's cot]	– **en barneseng** ehn <u>bah</u>·ner·sehng

You May Hear…

Må jeg bede om dit *pas/kreditkort*. mow yie beh ohm deet *pas/kreh·<u>deet</u>·kawd*	Your *passport/credit card*, please.
Udfyld venligst denne formular. <u>oodh</u>·fewl <u>vehn</u>·leesd <u>deh</u>·ner foh·moo·<u>lah</u>	Fill out this form.
Underskriv venligst her. <u>oa</u>·nah·sgreew <u>vehn</u>·leesd hehr	Sign here.

Price

How much per *night/week*?	**Hvad koster det per *nat/uge*?** vadh <u>kohs</u>·dah deh pehr *nad/<u>oo</u>·er*
Does the price include *breakfast/sales tax [VAT]*?	**Inkluderer prisen *morgenmad/moms*?** in·kloo·<u>deh</u>·ah <u>pree</u>·sern *<u>mawn</u>·madh/mawms*

Questions

Where's…?	**Hvor er…?** voar ehr…
– the bar	– **baren** <u>bah</u>·ern

Where's…?	Hvor er…? voar ehr…
– the restroom [toilet]	– toilettet toa·ee·<u>leh</u>·derdh
– elevator [lift]	– elevatoren eh·ler·<u>va</u>·tohn
Can I have…?	Kan jeg få…? kan yie fow…
– a blanket	– et tæppe eht <u>teh</u>·ber
– an iron	– et strygejern eht <u>strew</u>·er·yehrn
– a pillow	– en pude ehn <u>poo</u>·dher
– soap	– noget sæbe <u>noa</u>·erdh <u>say</u>·ber
– toilet paper	– noget toiletpapir <u>noa</u>·erdh toa·ee·<u>led</u>·pah·peer
– a towel	– et håndklæde eht <u>hawn</u>·kl<u>ay</u>·dher
Do you have an adapter for this?	Har I en adapter til denne her? har ee ehn a·<u>dahp</u>·tah til <u>deh</u>·ner hehr
How do I turn on the lights?	Hvordan tænder jeg lyset? voar·<u>dan</u> <u>tay</u>·ner yie <u>lew</u>·serdh
Can you wake me at…?	Kan du vække mig klokken…? kan doo <u>vay</u>·ger mie <u>klohg</u>·gehrn…
Can I have my things from the safe?	Må jeg få mine ting i boksen? mow yie fow <u>mee</u>·ner ting ee <u>bohk</u>·sern
Is there *any mail/a message* for me?	Er der *noget post/nogen beskeder* til mig? ehr dehr *<u>noa</u>·erdh pohst/<u>noa</u>·ern beh·<u>sgeh</u>·dhah* til mie

You May See…

SKUB/TRÆK	push/pull
TOILET	restroom [toilet]
BRUSER	shower
ELEVATOREN	elevator [lift]
TRAPPE	stairs

VASKERI	laundry
VIL IKKE FORSTYRRES	do not disturb
BRANDDØR	fire door
NØDUDGANG	emergency exit
MORGENVÆKNING	wake-up call

Problems

There's a problem.	**Der er et problem.** dehr ehr eht proa-<u>blehm</u>
I've lost my *key/key card*.	**Jeg har tabt *min nøgle/mit nøglekort*.** yie hah tahbd *meen <u>noi</u>-ler/meet <u>noi</u>-ler-kawd*
I've locked myself out of my room.	**Jeg har låst mig ude af mit værelse.** yie hah lowsd mie <u>oo</u>-dher a meet <u>vehrl</u>-ser
There's no *hot water/ toilet paper*.	**Der er ikke noget *varmt vand/ toiletpapir*.** dehr ehr ig-ger <u>noa</u>-erdh *van/toa-ee-<u>lehd</u>-pah-peer*
The room is dirty.	**Værelset er beskidt.** <u>vehrl</u>-serdh ehr beh-<u>skeed</u>
There are bugs in our room.	**Der er insekter på værelset.** dehr ehr in-<u>sehg</u>-tah paw <u>vehrl</u>-serd
...doesn't work.	**...er i uorden.** ...ehr ee <u>oo</u>-<u>oh</u>-dern
Can you fix...?	**Kan du reparere...?** kan doo reh-pah-<u>reh</u>-ah...
– the air conditioning	– **klimaanlægget** <u>klee</u>-ma-an-layg
– the fan	– **ventilatoren** vehn-tee-la-sho<u>an</u>
– the heat [heating]	– **varmen** <u>vah</u>-mern
– the light	– **lyset** <u>lew</u>-serdh
– the TV	– **fjernsynet** <u>fyehrn</u>-sew-nerdh
– the toilet	– **toilettet** toa-ee-<u>leh</u>-derdh
Can I get another room?	**Kan jeg få et andet værelse?** can yie fow eht <u>an</u>-erdh <u>vehrl</u>-ser

Danish electricity is generally 220 volts, though many camping sites also have 110-volt plugs available. British and American appliances will need an adapter.

Check-out

When do I have to check out?	**Hvornår skal jeg tjekke ud?** voar·<u>naw</u> skal yie <u>tyay</u>·ger oodh
Can I leave my bags here until…?	**Må jeg lade mine tasker stå her indtil…?** mow yie la <u>mee</u>·ner <u>tas</u>·gah stow hehr <u>in</u>·til…
Can I have *an itemized bill/a receipt*?	**Må jeg bede om en *udspecificeret regning/kvittering*?** mow yie beh ohm ehn oodh·speh·see·fee·<u>seh</u>·redh <u>rie</u>·ning/ kvee·<u>teh</u>·ring
I think there's a mistake in this bill.	**Jeg tror, der er en fejl i regningen.** yie troar dehr ehr ehn fiel ee <u>rie</u>·ning·ern
I'll pay *in cash/by credit card*.	**Jeg vil gerne betale *kontant/med kreditkort*.** yie vil <u>gehr</u>·ner beh·<u>ta</u>·ler kohn·<u>tant</u>/mehdh kreh·<u>deet</u>·kawd

In Denmark, **moms** (sales tax or value-added tax) and service charges are included in your bill in hotels and restaurants, in admissions charges and purchase prices as well as taxi fares. Tips may be given for outstanding service, but they are not necessary.

Renting ————

I've reserved *an apartment/a room*.	**Jeg har reserveret *en lejlighed/et værelse*.** yie hah reh·sah·<u>veh</u>·rerdh ehn <u>lie</u>·lee·hehdh/eht <u>vehrl</u>·ser
My name is…	**Mit navn er…** meet nown ehr…
Can I have the *key/ key card*?	**Må jeg bede om *nøglen/nøglekortet*?** mow yie beh ohm <u>noi</u>·lern/<u>noi</u>·ler·kaw·derdh

Are there...?	Findes der...? fin·ners dehr...
– dishes	– **spisestel** <u>spee</u>·ser·stehl
– pillows	– **puder** <u>poo</u>·dhah
– sheets	– **lagener** <u>la</u>·ner
– towels	– **håndklæder** <u>hawn</u>·klay·dhah
When/Where do I put out the trash [rubbish]?	*Hvornår/Hvor* skal jeg sætte skraldet ud? *voar·<u>naw</u>/voar* skal yie <u>seh</u>·der skrah·<u>lerdh</u> oodh
... is broken.	**...er i uorden.** ...ehr ee <u>oo</u>·oh·dern
How does...work?	**Hvordan fungerer...?** voar·<u>dan</u> fung·<u>geh</u>·rah...
– the air conditioner	– **klimaanlægget** <u>klee</u>·ma·an·lay·gerdh
– the dishwasher	– **opvaskemaskinen** <u>ohb</u>·va·sker·ma·s<u>kee</u>·nern
– the freezer	– **fryseren** fr<u>ew</u>·sern
– the heater	– **varmen** <u>vah</u>·mern
– the microwave	– **mikroovnen** <u>mee</u>·kroa·ow·nern
– the refrigerator	– **køleskabet** <u>kur</u>·ler·ska·berdh
– the stove	– **ovnen** <u>ow</u>·nern
– the washing machine	– **vaskemaskinen** <u>vas</u>·ger·ma·s<u>kee</u>·nern

Household Items

I need...	Jeg skal bruge... yie skal <u>broo</u>·er...
– an adapter	– **en adapter** ehn a·dahb·dah
– aluminum [kitchen] foil	– **aluminiumsfolie** a·loo·<u>mee</u>·nee·oums·<u>foal</u>·yer
– a bottle opener	– **en oplukker** ehn <u>ohb</u>·loa·ger
– a broom	– **en kost** ehn kowsd

I need...	Jeg skal bruge... yie skal <u>broo</u>·er...
– a can opener	– **en dåseåbner** ehn <u>dow</u>·ser·<u>owb</u>·nah
– cleaning supplies	– **rengøringsartikler** <u>rehn</u>·gur·rings·ah·teek·lah
– a corkscrew	– **en proptrækker** ehn <u>prohb</u>·tray·gah
– detergent	– **vaskemiddel** vas·ker·<u>mee</u>·dherl
– dishwashing liquid	– **opvaskemiddel** <u>ohb</u>·vas·ker·**mee**·dherl
– garbage [rubbish] bags	– **skraldeposer** <u>skrah</u>·ler·poa·sah
– a light bulb	– **en pære** ehn <u>pay</u>·ah
– matches	– **tændstikker** <u>tehn</u>·sti·kah
– a mop	– **en moppe** ehn <u>moh</u>·ber
– napkins	– **papirservietter** pah·<u>peer</u>·sehr·vee·<u>eh</u>·dah
– paper towels	– **papirhåndklæder** pah·<u>peer</u>·hawn·k**lay**·dhah
– plastic wrap [cling film]	– **plastfolie** <u>plast</u>·foal·yer
– scissors	– **en saks** ehn saks
– a vacuum cleaner	– **en støvsuger** ehn <u>sturw</u>·soo·ah

▶ For dishes and utensils, see page 62.

▶ For oven temperatures, see page 168.

Hostel

Do you have any places left for tonight?	**Har I nogen ledige pladser i nat?** hah ee <u>noa</u>·ern <u>leh</u>·dhi·yer <u>plas</u>·sah ee nad
Can I have...?	**Kan jeg få...?** kan yie fow...
– a *single/double* room	– **et *enkeltværelse/dobbeltværelse*** eht <u>ehn</u>·kerld·v**ehr**l·ser/<u>doh</u>·berld·v**ehr**l·ser
– a blanket	– **et tæppe** eht tay·ber
– a pillow	– **en pude** ehn <u>poo</u>·dher

– soap	– **sæbe** <u>say</u>·ber
– towels	– **håndklæder** hawn·klay·dhah
What time do you lock up?	**Hvornår lukker I for natten?** voar·<u>naw</u> <u>loa</u>·gah ee foh <u>nad</u>·dern

i
Known as **DANHOSTEL**, **Danmarks Vandrerhjem**, the Danish Youth Hostel Association operates official youth hostels throughout Denmark. You may request a private or shared room. The charge covers only the cost of the room; additional fees apply for bed linens and/or breakfast. Hostelling International (HI) cardholders are exempt from surcharges and receive special discounts. You may purchase HI membership cards on the spot.

Camping

Can we camp here?	**Kan vi campere her?** kan vee kahm·<u>peh</u>·ah hehr
Is there a campsite near here?	**Er der en campingplads i nærheden?** ehr dehr ehn <u>kahm</u>·ping·plas ee <u>nehr</u>·heh·dhern
What is the charge per *day/week*?	**Hvad koster det per *dag/uge*?** vadh <u>kohs</u>·dah deh pehr da/<u>oo</u>·er
Are there…?	**Er der…?** ehr dehr…
– cooking facilities	– **køkkenfaciliteter** <u>kur</u>·ken·fa·see·lee·teh·dah
– electrical outlets	– **stikkontakter** <u>stik</u>·kohn·tahg·dah
– laundry facilities	– **vaskerum** <u>vas</u>·ger·roam
– showers	– **brusebad** <u>broo</u>·ser·badh
– tents for rent [hire]	– **telte til leje** <u>tehl</u>·der til <u>lie</u>·er
Where can I empty the chemical toilet?	**Hvor kan jeg tømme det kemiske toilet?** voar kan yie <u>tur</u>·mer deh <u>keh</u>·mis·ger toa·ee·<u>lehd</u>

You May See...

DRIKKEVAND	drinking water
CAMPING FORBUDT	no camping
BÅLTÆNDING/GRILLNING FORBUDT	no *fires/barbecues*

▶ For household items, see page 43.

▶ For dishes, utensils and kitchen tools, see page 62.

Internet and Communications

Essential

Where's an internet cafe?	**Hvor ligger der en internetcafé?** voar <u>li</u>·gah dehr ehn in·tah·neht·ca·feh
Can I *access the internet here/check e-mail*?	**Kan jeg gå på *internettet herfra/tjekke min e-mail*?** kan yie gow paw in·tah·neh·derdh <u>hehr</u>·frah/<u>tjay</u>·ker meen **ee**·mail
How much per *hour/ half hour*?	**Hvor meget koster det per *time/halve time*?** voar <u>mie</u>·erdh <u>kohs</u>·dah deh pehr **tee**·mer/<u>hal</u>·ver **tee**·mer
How do I *connect/ log on*?	**Hvordan *kobler/logger* jeg mig på?** voar·<u>dan</u> <u>kohb</u>·lah/<u>lohg</u>·ah yie mie paw
I'd like a phone card, please.	**Jeg vil gerne have et telefonkort, tak.** yie vil <u>gehr</u>·ner ha eht teh·ler·<u>**foan**</u>·kawd tahk
Can I have your phone number?	**Kan jeg få dit telefonnummer?** kan yie fow deet teh·ler·<u>**foan**</u>·noa·mer
Here's my *number/ e-mail address*.	**Her er *mit telefonnumer/min e-mail-adresse*.** hehr ehr *meet teh·ler·<u>**foan**</u>·noa·mer/ meen **ee**·mail·a·drah·ser*

Call me.	**Ring til mig.** ring til mie
E-mail me.	**Send mig en e-mail.** sehn mie ehn <u>ee</u>·mail
Hello. This is…	**Hallo. Det er…** ha·<u>loa</u> deh ehr…
I'd like to speak to…	**Jeg vil gerne tale med…** yie vil <u>gehr</u>·ner <u>ta</u>·ler medh…
Can you repeat that?	**Kan du gentage det?** kan doo <u>gehn</u>·ta deh
I'll call back later.	**Jeg ringer tilbage senere.** yie <u>ring</u>·ah til·<u>ba</u>·yer <u>seh</u>·nah
Bye.	**Farvel.** fah·<u>vehl</u>
Where's the post office?	**Hvor ligger posthuset?** voar <u>li</u>·gah <u>pohsd</u>·**hoo**·serdh
I'd like to send this to…	**Jeg vil gerne sende dette til…** yie vil <u>gehr</u>·ner <u>seh</u>·ner <u>deh</u>·der til…

Computer, Internet and E-mail

Where's an internet cafe?	**Hvor ligger der en internetcafé?** voar li·gah dehr ehn <u>in</u>·tah·neht·ca·f**eh**
Does it have wireless internet?	**Har den trådløst internet?** hah dehn <u>trowdh</u>·lurst <u>in</u>·tah·net
How do I turn the computer *on/off*?	**Hvordan *tænder/slukker* jeg for computeren?** voar·<u>dan</u> *tay·nah/<u>sloa</u>·gah* yie foh cohm·<u>pew</u>·dern
Can I…?	**Kan jeg…?** kan yie…
– access the internet here	– **gå på internettet herfra** gow paw <u>in</u>·tah·neh·derdh <u>hehr</u>·frah
– check e-mail	– **tjekke min e-mail** <u>tjay</u>·ker meen <u>ee</u>·mail
– print	– **printe** <u>prin</u>·ter
How much per *hour/half hour*?	**Hvor meget koster det per *time/halve time*?** voar <u>mie</u>·erdh <u>kohs</u>·dah deh pehr *<u>tee</u>·mer/<u>hal</u>·ver <u>tee</u>·mer*

How do I...?	**Hvordan....?** voar·<u>dan</u>...
– connect/disconnect	**– kobler jeg mig *på/fra*** <u>kohb</u>·lah yie mie *paw/frah*
– log *on/off*	**– logger jeg *på/af*** <u>lohg</u>·ah yie *paw/a*
– type this symbol	**– indtaster jeg dette symbol** <u>in</u>·tas·dah yie <u>deh</u>·der sewm·<u>boal</u>
What's your e-mail?	**Hvad er din e-mail adresse?** vadh ehr deen <u>ee</u>·mail·a·drah·ser
My e-mail is...	**Min e-mail adresse er...** meen <u>ee</u>·mail·a·drah·ser ehr...

You May See...

E-MAIL	e-mail
FORLAD	exit
HJÆLP	help
INSTANT MESSENGER	instant messenger
INTERNET	internet
LOG IND	login
NY (BESKED)	new (message)
UDSKRIV	print
BRUGERNAVN/ADGANGSKODE	username/password
TRÅDLØS INTERNETFORBINDELSE	wireless internet

Phone

A phone card, please.	**Jeg vil gerne have et telefonkort, tak.** yie vil gehr·ner ha ehd teh·ler·<u>foan</u>·kawd tahk
How much?	**Hvor meget koster det?** voar <u>mie</u>·erdh <u>kohs</u>·dah deh
My phone doesn't work here.	**Min telefon virker ikke her.** meen teh·ler·<u>foan</u> <u>veer</u>·gah <u>ig</u>·ger hehr
What's the *area/country* code for...?	**Hvad er *områdenummeret/landekoden* for...?** vadh ehr <u>ohm</u>·*row·dhe·noa·mahrdh/la·ner·<u>koa</u>·dher* foh...
What's the number for Information?	**Hvad er nummeret til nummeroplysningen?** vadh ehr <u>noa</u>·mahrdh til <u>noa</u>·mah·ohb·<u>lews</u>·ning·ern
I'd like the number for...	**Jeg vil gerne bede om nummeret til...** yie vil <u>gehr</u>·ner beh ohm <u>noa</u>·mahrdh til...
Can I have your number?	**Må jeg få dit nummer?** mow yie fow deet <u>noa</u>·mah

My number is... **Mit nummer er...** meet <u>noa</u>·mah ehr...

▶For numbers, see page 162.

Call me. **Ring venligst til mig.** ring <u>vehn</u>·leest til mie

Text me. **Send mig venligst en tekstbesked.** sehn mie <u>vehn</u>·leest ehn <u>tehkst</u>·beh·skehdh

I'll call you. **Jeg ringer til dig.** yie <u>ring</u>·ah til die

I'll text you. **Jeg sender dig en tekstbesked.** yie <u>sehn</u>·ah die ehn <u>tehkst</u>·beh·skehdh

On the Phone

Hello. This is... **Hallo. Det er...** ha·<u>loa</u> deh ehr...

I'd like to speak to... **Jeg vil gerne tale med...** yie vil <u>gehr</u>·ner <u>ta</u>·ler mehdh...

Extension... **Lokal...** loa·<u>kal</u>...

Speak *louder/more slowly*, please. **Vær rar og tal *lidt højere/lidt langsommere.*** vehr rah ow <u>ta</u>·ler *lit <u>hoi</u>·ah/lit <u>lang</u>·sohm·ah*

Can you repeat that? **Kan du gentage det?** kan doo <u>gehn</u>·ta deh

I'll call back later. **Jeg ringer tilbage senere.** yie <u>ring</u>·ah til·<u>ba</u>·yer <u>seh</u>·nah

Bye. **Farvel.** fah·<u>vehl</u>

▶For business travel, see page 139.

You May Hear...

Hvem er det? vehm ehr deh — Who's calling?

Vær rar og vent. vehr rah ow <u>vehn</u>·der — Hold on.

Han/Hun **kan ikke komme til telefonen.** *han/hoon* kan <u>ig</u>·ger <u>koh</u>·mer til teh·ler·<u>foa</u>·nern — *He/She* can't come to the phone.

Ønsker du at lægge en besked? <u>urn</u>·sgah doo ad <u>lay</u>·ger ehn beh·<u>skehdh</u> — Would you like to leave a message?

Kan *han/hun* ringe tilbage til dig? kan *han/hoon* <u>ring</u>·er til·<u>ba</u>·yer til die — Can *he/she* call you back?

Hvad er dit telefonnummer? vadh ehr deet teh·ler·<u>foan</u>·noa·mah — What's your number?

Fax

Can I *send/receive* a fax here?
Kan jeg *sende/modtage* en fax her? kan yie *<u>sehn</u>·ner/<u>moadh</u>·ta* ehn fahks hehr

What's the fax number?
Hvad er faxnummeret? vadh ehr <u>fahks</u>·noa·mahrdh

Fax this to…
Fax venligst dette til… fahks <u>vehn</u>·leesd <u>deh</u>·ter til…

In Denmark, public phones either accept coins or prepaid phone cards. For coin-operated phones, once the line is engaged—even if it is busy—your coin will not be returned, so start with a low denomination coin. Prepaid phone cards can be purchased in post offices and kiosks. Keep in mind that the price per call from a public phone is twice that from a private line. Some kiosks allow you to make calls with a cheaper international rate using prepaid phone cards. Calls can also be made from the TelecomCenter at Central Train Station in Copenhagen.

Important telephone numbers:
emergencies, 112
information, 118
operator assistance, 113

To call the U.S. or Canada from Denmark, dial 00 + 1 + area code + phone number. To call the U.K., dial 00 + 44 + area code (minus the first 0) + phone number.

Post Office

Where's the *post office/mailbox [postbox]*?	**Hvor *ligger posthuset/er postkassen*?** voar li·gah <u>pohst</u>·h**oo**·serdh/ehr <u>pohst</u>·ka·sern
A stamp for this *letter/ postcard*, please.	**Jeg vil gerne have et frimærke til dette *brev/postkort*, tak.** Yie vil <u>gehr</u>·ne ha eht <u>free</u>·mehr·ker til <u>deh</u>·der brehw/<u>pohst</u>·kawd tahk
How much?	**Hvor meget koster det?** voar <u>mie</u>·erdh <u>kohs</u>·dah deh
I'd like to send this package by *airmail/ express*.	**Jeg vil gerne sende denne pakke med *luftpost/ekspres*.** yie vil <u>gehr</u>·ner <u>sehn</u>·ner <u>deh</u>·ner pah·ker mehdh <u>loaft</u>·pohst/<u>ehks</u>·<u>prehs</u>
Can I have receipt?	**Kan jeg få en kvittering?** kan yie fow ehn kvee·<u>teh</u>·ring

The regular hours of operation of post offices in Denmark are Monday to Friday from 10 a.m. to 5:30 p.m. and Saturday 10 a.m. to 1 p.m.; hours in the provinces may vary. Mailboxes are red and, like post office signs, display an embossed crown-and-arrow logo and **POST** in white.

▼ Food

Essential

Can you recommend a good *restaurant/ bar*?	**Kan du anbefale en god *restaurant/ bar*?** kan doo <u>an</u>·beh·**fa**·ler ehn goadh reh·stoa·<u>rang</u>/b**ah**
Is there *a traditional Danish/ an inexpensive* restaurant nearby?	**Ligger der en *typisk dansk/ikke så dyr* restaurant i nærheden?** <u>li</u>·gah der ehn *<u>tew</u>·peesk dansk/<u>ig</u>·ger saw dewr* reh·stoa·<u>rang</u> ee <u>nehr</u>·**h**eh·dhern
A table for…, please.	**Et bord til…tak.** eht boar til…tahk
Can we sit…?	**Må vi sidde…?** mow vee <u>si</u>·dher…
– here/there	**– her/der** hehr/dehr
– outside	**– udenfor** <u>oo</u>·dhern·foh
– at a non-smoking table	**– ved et bord for ikke-rygere** vehdh eht boar foh <u>ig</u>·ger·<u>rew</u>·ah
I'm waiting for someone.	**Jeg venter på nogen.** yie <u>vehn</u>·dah paw <u>noa</u>·ern
Where is the restroom [toilet]?	**Hvor er toilettet?** voar ehr toa·ee·<u>leh</u>·derdh
I'd like a menu, please.	**Jeg vil gerne bede om et menukort, tak.** yie vil <u>gehr</u>·ner beh ohm eht meh·<u>new</u>·kawd tahk
What do you recommend?	**Hvad kan du anbefale?** vadh kan doo <u>an</u>·beh·**fa**·ler
I'd like…	**Jeg vil gerne have…** yie vil <u>gehr</u>·ner ha…
Some more, please.	**Jeg vil gerne have lidt mere, tak.** yie vil <u>gehr</u>·ner ha lit <u>meh</u>·ah tahk
Enjoy your meal.	**Velbekomme.** <u>vehl</u>·beh·koh·mer

Can I have the check [bill]?	**Kan jeg få regningen?** kan yie fow <u>rie</u>·ning·ern
Is service included?	**Er drikkepenge inkluderet?** ehr <u>drig</u>·ger·pehng·er in·kloo·<u>deh</u>·rerdh
Can I pay by credit card?	**Kan jeg betale med kreditkort?** kan yie beh·<u>ta</u>·ler mehdh kreh·<u>deet</u>·kawd
Can I have a receipt?	**Kan jeg få en kvittering?** kan yie fow ehn kvee·<u>teh</u>·ring
Thank you.	**Tak.** tahk

Restaurant Types

Can you recommend…?	**Kan du anbefale…?** kan doo <u>an</u>·beh·<u>fa</u>·ler…
– a restaurant	– **en restaurant** ehn reh·stoa·<u>rang</u>
– a bar	– **en bar** ehn b**ah**
– a cafe	– **en café** ehn ca·<u>feh</u>
– a fast-food place	– **en burgerbar** ehn <u>bur</u>·gah·bah

Reservations and Questions

I'd like to reserve a table…	**Jeg vil gerne bestille et bord…** yie vil <u>gehr</u>·ner beh·<u>stil</u>·ler eht boar…
– for two	– **til to** til toa
– for this evening	– **til i aften** til ee <u>ahf</u>·tern
– for tomorrow at…	– **til i morgen klokken…** til ee mawn <u>kloh</u>·gehrn…
A table for two, please.	**Et bord til to, tak.** eht boar til toa tahk
We have a reservation.	**Vi har en reservation.** vee hah ehn reh·sah·va·<u>shoan</u>

My name is…	**Mit navn er…** meet nown ehr…
Can we sit…?	**Må vi sidde…?** mow vee si·dher…
– here/there	**– her/der** hehr/dehr
– outside	**– udenfor** oo·dhern·foh
– at a non-smoking table	**– ved et bord for ikke-rygere** vehdh eht boar for ig·ger·rew·ah
– by the window	**– ved vinduet** vehdh vin·doo·erdh
Where is the restroom [toilet]?	**Hvor er toilettet?** voar ehr toa·ee·leh·derdh

You May Hear…

Har du bestilt et bord? hah doo beh·stild eht boar	Do you have a reservation?
Til hvor mange? til voar mang·er	For how many?
Ryger eller ikke-ryger? rew·ah ehl·lah ig·ger rew·ah	Smoking or non-smoking?
Er I klar til at bestille? ehr ee klah til ad beh·stil·ler	Are you ready to order?
Hvad kunne I tænke jer? vadh koo·ner ee tehn·ker yehr	What would you like?
Jeg kan anbefale… yie kan an·beh·fa·ler…	I recommend…
Velbekomme. vehl·beh·koh·mer	Enjoy your meal.

Ordering

Waiter/Waitress!	**Tjener/Frøken!** tyeh·nah/frur·kern
We're ready to order.	**Vi er klar til bestille.** vee ehr klah til ad beh·stil·ler
May I see the wine list?	**Må jeg bede om en vinliste?** mow yie beh ohm ehn veen·lis·der

56

I'd like...	**Jeg vil gerne have...** yie vil <u>gehr</u>·ner ha...
– a bottle of...	**– en flaske...** ehn <u>flas</u>·ger...
– a carafe of...	**– en karaffel...** ehn ka·<u>rah</u>·ferl...
– a glass of...	**– et glas...** eht glas...

▶For alcoholic and non-alcoholic drinks, see page 77.

Can I have a menu?	**Må jeg bede om et menukort?** mow yie beh ohm <u>eht</u> meh·<u>new</u>·kawd
Do you have...?	**Er der...?** ehr dehr...
– a menu in English	**– et menukort på engelsk** eht meh·<u>new</u>·kawd paw <u>ehng</u>·erlsk
– a fixed-price menu	**– et dagens tilbud** eht <u>da</u>·erns <u>til</u>·boodh
– a children's menu	**– en børnemenu** ehn <u>bur</u>·ner·meh·new
What do you recommend?	**Hvad kan du anbefale?** vadh kan doo <u>an</u>·beh·<u>fa</u>·ler
What's this?	**Hvad er det?** vadh ehr deh

What's in it?	**Hvad er der i?** vadh ehr da ee
Is it spicy?	**Er det krydret?** ehr deh <u>krewdh</u>·rerdh
It's to go [take away].	**Jeg tager det med mig.** yie tah deh mehdh mie

Cooking Methods

baked	**bagt** bahgt
boiled	**kogt** kohgt
braised	**grydestegt** <u>grew</u>·dher·stehgt
breaded	**paneret** pa·<u>neh</u>·rerdh
creamed	**tilberedt med fløde** <u>til</u>·beh·rehd mehdh <u>flur</u>·dher
diced	**skåret i terninger** sk<u>aw</u>·rerdh ee <u>tehr</u>·ning·ah
fileted	**fileteret** fee·leh·<u>teh</u>·rerdh
fried	**stegt** stehgt
grilled	**grillet** <u>gree</u>·lerdh
poached	**pocheret** poa·<u>sheh</u>·rerdh
roasted	**ovnstegt** own·stehgt
sautéed	**sauteret** saw·<u>teh</u>·rerdh
smoked	**røget** <u>roi</u>·erdh
steamed	**dampet** <u>dahm</u>·berdh
stewed	**stuvet** <u>stoo</u>·erdh
stuffed	**farseret** fah·<u>seh</u>·rerdh

Special Requirements

I'm…	**Jeg…** yie…
– diabetic	– **har sukkersyge** hah <u>soa</u>·gah·s<u>ew</u>·er
– lactose intolerant	– **er laktoseallergiker** ehr lahk·<u>toa</u>·ser·a·lehr·gee·gar
– vegetarian	– **er vegetar** ehr veh·geh·<u>tah</u>

58

I'm allergic to…	**Jeg kan ikke tåle…** yie kan ig·ger <u>tow</u>·ler…
I can't eat…	**Jeg kan ikke spise…** yie kan ig·ger <u>spee</u>·ser…
– dairy	– **mælkeprodukter** <u>mehl</u>·ker·proa·doag·dah
– gluten	– **gluten** <u>gloo</u>·dern
– nuts	– **nødder** <u>nur</u>·dhah
– pork	– **svinekød** <u>svee</u>·ner·kurdh
– shellfish	– **skaldyr** <u>skal</u>·dewr
– spicy foods	– **krydret mad** <u>krewdh</u>·rerdh madh
– wheat	– **hvede** <u>veh</u>·dher
Is it *halal/kosher*?	**Er det *halal/kosher*?** ehr deh ha·<u>lal</u>/<u>koh</u>·sher

Dining with Kids

Do you have children's portions?	**Serverer I mad i børneportioner?** sehr·<u>veh</u>·ah ee madh ee <u>bur</u>·ner·poh·shoa·nah
A *highchair/child's seat*, please.	**Jeg vil gerne bede om *en høj stol/et barnesæde*, tak.** yie vil <u>gehr</u>·ner beh ohm *ehn hoi stoal/eht <u>bah</u>·ner·<u>say</u>·dher* tahk
Where can I *feed/change* the baby?	**Hvor kan jeg *made/skifte* babyen?** voar kan yie *<u>ma</u>·dher/<u>skeef</u>·der* bay·bee·ern
Can you warm this?	**Kan du opvarme dette?** kan doo <u>ohb</u>·vah·mer <u>deh</u>·deh

▶For travel with children, see page 141.

Complaints

How much longer will our food be?	**Hvor lang tid tager det, før maden er klar?** voar lahng teedh tah deh fur <u>ma</u>·dhern ehr klah
We can't wait any longer.	**Vi kan ikke vente længere.** vee kan ig·ger <u>vehn</u>·der <u>layng</u>·ah
We're leaving.	**Vi går.** vee gaw

59

I didn't order this.	**Det har jeg ikke bestilt.** deh hah yie <u>ig</u>·ger <u>beh</u>·stilt
I ordered…	**Jeg bad om…** yie badh ohm…
I can't eat this.	**Jeg kan ikke spise det her.** yie kan <u>ig</u>·ger <u>spee</u>·ser deh hehr
This is too…	**Det her er for…** deh hehr ehr foh…
– cold/hot	**– koldt/varmt** kohlt/vahmt
– salty/spicy	**– saltet/krydret** <u>sal</u>·terdh/<u>krewdh</u>·rerdh
– tough/bland	**– sejt/har ingen smag** sied/hah <u>ing</u>·ern sma
This isn't *clean/fresh*.	**Det her er ikke *rent/frisk*.** deh hehr ehr <u>ig</u>·ger *rehnt/frisk*

Paying

I'd like the check [bill].	**Må jeg bede om regningen.** mow yie beh ohm <u>rie</u>·ning·ern
We'd like to pay separately.	**Vi vil gerne betale hver for sig.** vee vil <u>gehr</u>·ner beh·<u>ta</u>·ler vehr foh sie
It's all together.	**Vi vil gerne betale samlet.** vee vil <u>gehr</u>·ner beh·<u>ta</u>·ler <u>sahm</u>·lerdh
Is service included?	**Er drikkepenge inkluderet?** ehr <u>drig</u>·ger·pehng·er in·kloo·<u>deh</u>·erdh
What's this amount for?	**Hvad dækker dette beløb?** vadh <u>day</u>·gah <u>deh</u>·der beh·<u>lurb</u>
I didn't have that. I had…	**Det har jeg ikke bestilt. Jeg fik…** deh hah yie <u>ig</u>·ger beh·<u>stilt</u> yie feek…
Can I pay by credit card?	**Kan jeg betale med kreditkort?** kan yie beh·<u>ta</u>·ler mehdh kreh·<u>deet</u>·kawd
Can I have an *itemized bill/a receipt*?	**Må jeg bede om *en udspecificeret regning/en kvittering*?** mow yie beh ohm *ehn <u>oodh</u>·speh·see·fee·<u>seh</u>·ahdh <u>rie</u>·ning/ehn kvee·<u>teh</u>·ring*
That was a very good meal.	**Det var meget lækker mad.** deh vah <u>mie</u>·erdh <u>lehg</u>·gah madh

> **Moms** (sales tax or value-added tax) and service charges
> are already included in your final bill in restaurants. Tips for
> outstanding service are a matter of personal choice.

Market

Where are the *carts* [trolleys]/baskets? | **Hvor er *vognene/kurvene*?** voar ehr *vow*·ner·ner/*koor*·ver·ner

Where is...? | **Hvor er...?** voar ehr...

▶ For food items, see page 81.

I'd like some of *that/those*. | **Jeg vil gerne have *noget af det/nogle af dem.*** yie vil *gehr*·ner ha *noa*·erdh a deh/*noa*·ler a dehm

Can I taste it? | **Må jeg smage det?** mow yie *sma*·yer deh

I'd like... | **Jeg vil gerne have...** yie vil *gehr*·ner ha...

– a *kilo/half-kilo* of... | **– et *kilo/halvt kilo*...** eht *kee*·loa/halt *kee*·lo...

– a *liter/half-liter* of... | **– en *liter/halv liter*...** ehn *lee*·dah/hal *lee*·dah...

– a piece of... | **– et stykke...** eht *stur*·ger...

– a slice of... | **– en skive...** ehn *skee*·ver...

▶ For conversion tables, see page 167.

More/Less than that. | ***Mere/Mindre* end det.** *meh*·ah/*min*·drah ehn deh

How much? | **Hvor meget koster det?** voar *mie*·erdh *kos*·dah deh

Where do I pay? | **Hvor kan jeg betale?** voar kan yie beh·*ta*·ler

Can I have a bag? | **Kan jeg få en bærepose?** kan yie fow ehn *bay*·rah·*poa*·ser

I'm being helped. | **Jeg bliver ekspederet.** yie *blee*·vah ehks·peh·*deh*·rahdh

Kan jeg hjælpe dig? kan yie <u>yehl</u>·per die	Can I help you?
Hvad skulle det være? vadh skoo deh <u>vay</u>·ah	What would you like?
Skulle der være andet? skoo dah <u>vay</u>·ah <u>a</u>·nerdh	Anything else?
Det bliver...kroner. deh bleer...<u>kroa</u>·nah	That's...kroner.

In Denmark, there are a few supermarket chains in addition to many local markets located in every city and town. Not all supermarkets accept international credit cards; some accept only **Dankort** (the special Danish equivalent of credit and debit cards). So remember to bring cash when you go shopping for groceries.

You May See...

MINDST HOLDBAR TIL...	best if used by...
KALORIER	calories
FEDTFRI	fat free
OPBEVARES I KØLESKAB	keep refrigerated
SIDSTE SALGSDATO	sell by
EGNET FOR VEGETARER	suitable for vegetarians

Dishes, Utensils and Kitchen Tools

bottle opener	**oplukker** <u>ohb</u>·loag·gah
bowls	**skåle** <u>skow</u>·ler

can opener	**dåseåbner** <u>dow</u>·ser·ow·bnah
corkscrew	**proptrækker** <u>prohb</u>·treh·kah
cups	**kopper** <u>koh</u>·bah
forks	**gafler** <u>gahf</u>·lah
frying pan	**stegepande** <u>stie</u>·yer·pa·ner
glasses	**glas** glas
knives	**knive** <u>knee</u>·ver
measuring *cup/* *spoon*	**målekrus/måleske** <u>mow</u>·ler·kroos/ <u>mow</u>·ler·skeh
napkins	**servietter** sehr·vee·<u>eh</u>·dah
plates	**tallerkner** ta·<u>lehrk</u>·nah
pot	**gryde** <u>grew</u>·dher
saucepan	**kasserolle** ka·ser·<u>rohl</u>·ler
spatula	**spatel** <u>spa</u>·derl
spoons	**skeer** <u>skeh</u>·ah

Meals

i **Morgenmad** (breakfast) is usually eaten quite early, since school and work often begin at 8 a.m. A typical breakfast includes buttered bread, **skæreost** (sliced cheese), creamy white cheese like Havarti, jam and coffee. **Frokost** (lunch) is often a simple meal of buttered bread and spreads. **Aftensmad** (dinner) begins at about 6 p.m. and is the main meal, as well as the only hot meal, of the day. Dinner may include several courses or may simply be a hearty soup followed by dessert.

Breakfast

appelsinjuice ah·berl·<u>seen</u>·djoos	orange juice
appelsinmarmelade ah·berl·<u>seen</u>·mah·mer·**la**·dher	orange marmalade
bacon og æg <u>bay</u>·kohn ow ayg	bacon and eggs
brød brurdh	bread
blødkogt/hårdkogt æg <u>blurdh</u>·kohgd/ <u>haw</u>·kohgd ayg	*soft-/hard*-boiled egg
grapefrugtjuice <u>grayb</u>·froagt·djoos	grapefruit juice
havregrød <u>how</u>·rah·grurdh	oatmeal
honning <u>hoh</u>·ning	honey
kaffe… <u>kah</u>·fer…	coffee…
– kaffeinfri kah·feh·**een**·free	– decaffeinated
– med mælk mehdh mehlk	– with milk
– sort soart	– black
(kold/varm) mælk (kohl/vahm) mehlk	(cold/hot) milk
omelet oa·mer·<u>leht</u>	omelet
pandekager <u>pa</u>·ner·ka·yah	pancakes
pølser <u>purl</u>·sah	sausage
ristet brød <u>ris</u>·terdh brurdh	toast
rundstykker <u>roan</u>·stur·gah	rolls
røræg <u>rur</u>·ayg	scrambled eggs
smør smur	butter
spejlæg <u>spiel</u>·ayg	fried eggs
skinke og æg <u>skin</u>·ger ow ayg	ham and eggs
syltetøj <u>sewl</u>·der·toi	jam

I'd like…	**Jeg vil gerne have…** yie vil <u>gehr</u>·ner ha…
More…please.	**Mere…tak.** <u>meh</u>·ah…tahk

te med *mælk/citron* teh mehdh *mehlk/see·troan*	tea with *milk/lemon*
varm chokolade vahm shoa·koa·**la**·dher	hot chocolate
yoghurt yoo·goord	yogurt

Appetizers [Starters]

ansjoser an·**shoa**·sah	anchovies
artiskokker ah·tees·**koh**·gah	artichokes
aspargeshoveder a·**spahs**·hoah·dhah	asparagus tips
champignoner sham·pin·yong	mushrooms
fyldte tomater fewl·der toa·**ma**·dah	stuffed tomatoes
gåselever gow·ser·lehw·ah	goose liver
kaviar ka·vee·**ah**	caviar
(marineret/røget) makrel (mah·**ree**·n**eh**·rahdh/roi·erdh) **ma**·krehl	(marinated/smoked) mackerel
muslinger moos·ling·ah	mussels
oliven (fyldte) oa·**lee**·vern (fewl·der)	(stuffed) olives
radiser rah·dee·sah	radishes
rollmops rohl·mops	pickled herring [rollmops]
***røget/graved* laks** roi·erdh/grah·verdh lahks	*smoked/cured* salmon
salat sa·lat	salad
saltkød sahlt·kurdh	salted beef slices
sild med løg seel mehdh loi	herring with onion
sildesalat see·ler·sa·lat	herring salad

With/Without…	**Med/Uden…** mehdh/**oo**·dhern…
I can't have…	**Jeg må ikke spise…** yie mow **ig**·ger **spee**·ser…

skinke skin·ger	ham
spegepølse spi·er·purl·ser	salami
østers urs·dahs	oysters
ål (i gelé) owl (ee sheh·leh)	(jellied) eel

Soup

aspargessuppe a·spahs·soa·per	asparagus soup
champignonsuppe sham·pin·yong·soa·per	mushroom soup
frugtsuppe froagt·soa·per	dried fruit soup, served chilled or hot
gule ærter goo·ler ehr·dah	split-pea soup with salt pork
hønsekødsuppe hurn·ser·kurdhs·soa·per	chicken and vegetable soup
hummersuppe hoa·mah·soa·per	lobster chowder
klar suppe med boller og grønsager klah soa·per mehdh boh·lah ow grurn·sa·yah	vegetable soup with meatballs
kråsesuppe krow·ser·soa·per	sweet-sour chicken giblets soup
labskoves lahb·sgows	hearty stew made with beef, potatoes, carrots and onions
æblesuppe ay·bler·soa·per	apple soup
ægte skildpaddesuppe ayg·der skil·pa·dher·soa·per	turtle soup
øllebrød ur·ler·brurdh	soup of rye bread cooked with Danish beer, sugar and lemon

I'd like...	**Jeg vil gerne have...** yie vil gehr·ner ha...
More...please.	**Mere...tak.** meh·ah...tahk

> Soup is, on many occasions, a meal on its own. If you'd like to try a traditional soup, order **aspargessuppe** (asparagus soup), **gule ærter** (split-pea soup), **frugtsuppe** (fruit soup) or chicken soup **med boller** (with meatballs).

Fish and Seafood

aborre a·bohr	perch
ansjoser an·shoa·sah	anchovies
blåmuslinger blaw·moos·ling·ah	mussels
forel foh·rehl	trout
gedde geh·dher	pike
helleflynder heh·ler·flur·nah	halibut
hummer hoa·mah	lobster
karpe kah·per	carp
krebs krehbs	crab
laks lahks	salmon
makrel ma·krehl	mackerel
pighvar peeg·vah	turbot
rejer rie·ah	shrimp [prawns]
rogn rown	roe
rødspætte rurdh·spay·der	plaice
sardiner sah·dee·nah	sardine
sild seel	herring
skrubbe skroa·ber	flounder
store rejer stoa·ah rie·ah	jumbo shrimp [prawns]

With/Without…	**Med/Uden…** mehdh/**oo**·dhern…
I can't have…	**Jeg må ikke spise…** yie mow ig·ger spee·ser…

stør stur	sturgeon
søtunge <u>sur</u>·toang·er	sole
torsk toh<u>sk</u>	cod
tunfisk <u>toon</u>·fisk	tuna
ørred <u>ur</u>·erdh	trout
østers <u>urs</u>·dahs	oysters
ål owl	eel

Meat and Poultry

and an	duck
bacon <u>bay</u>·kohn	bacon
blodpølse <u>bloadh</u>·purl·ser	black pudding
brisler <u>brees</u>·lah	sweetbreads
due <u>doo</u>·er	pigeon
dyrekød <u>dew</u>·er·kurdh	venison
fasan fa·<u>san</u>	pheasant
forloren skildpadde foh·<u>loarn</u> <u>skil</u>·pa·dher	"mock turtle": a very traditional Danish dish consisting of meat from a calf's head with meatballs and fish balls
frikadeller fri·ka·<u>deh</u>·lah	small meat patties
fårekød <u>faw</u>·er·kurdh	mutton
grisehoved/grisetæer <u>gree</u>·ser·hoa·wedh/ <u>gree</u>·ser·tehr	pig's *head/feet*

I'd like…	**Jeg vil gerne have…** yie vil <u>gehr</u>·ner ha…
More…please.	**Mere…tak.** <u>meh</u>·ah…tahk

grydesteg <u>grew</u>·dher·stie	pot roast
gås gows	goose
hakkebøf <u>hah</u>·ker·burf	ground beef patty
hamburgerryg <u>hahm</u>·boh·rurg	smoked, salted pork with cucumber sauce
hare <u>hah</u>·rer	hare
kalkun kal·<u>koon</u>	turkey
kalvebrissel <u>kal</u>·ver·bree·serl	veal cutlet
kalvekød <u>kal</u>·ver·kurdh	veal
kanin ka·<u>neen</u>	rabbit
koldt kødpålæg kohlt <u>kurdh</u>·paw·laygh	cold cuts
kylling <u>kew</u>·ling	chicken
kødboller <u>kurdh</u>·boh·lah	small meatballs, usually served in soup or with pasta
lam lahm	lamb
lever <u>leh</u>·wah	liver
medisterpølse meh·<u>dees</u>·dah·purl·ser	spiced pork sausage
oksehale <u>ohk</u>·ser·ha·ler	oxtail
oksekød <u>ohk</u>·ser·kurdh	beef
oksesteg <u>ohk</u>·ser·stie	roast beef
pattegris <u>pa</u>·der·grees	suckling pig
perlehøne <u>pehr</u>·ler·hur·ner	guinea fowl
pølse <u>purl</u>·sah	sausage
rensdyr <u>rehns</u>·dewr	reindeer

With/Without…	**Med/Uden…** mehdh/<u>oo</u>·dhern…	
I can't have…	**Jeg må ikke spise…** yie mow <u>ig</u>·ger <u>spee</u>·ser…	

skinke skin·ger	ham
sprængt oksebryst sprehngt ohk·ser·brurst	boiled, salted brisket of beef
svinekød svee·ner·kurdh	pork
ung and oang an	duckling
vagtel vahg·derl	quail
vildsvin veel·sveen	wild boar

rare	**letstegt** leht·stehgt
medium	**medium meh**·dee·oam
well-done	**gennemstegt** geh·nerm·stehgt

Danish Sandwiches: Smørrebrød

brød brurdh	bread
bøftartar burf·tah·tah	beef tartare
franskbrød frahnsk·brurdh	white bread
fuldkornsbrød fool·koarns·brurdh	whole-grain bread
kalvekød kal·ver·kurdh	veal
kaviar ka·vee·ah	caviar
laks lahks	salmon
leverpaté leh·wah·pa·teh	liver paté
oksesteg ohk·ser·stie	roast beef
ost oast	cheese
pumpernikkel-brød poom·pah·ni·kerl·brurdh	pumpernickel bread

I'd like…	**Jeg vil gerne have…** yie vil gehr·ner ha…
More…please.	**Mere…tak.** meh·ah…tahk

rejer <u>rie</u>·ah	shrimp
rogn rown	cod roe
rugbrød <u>roo</u>·brurdh	rye bread
sild… seel…	herring…
– **røget** <u>roi</u>·erdh	– smoked
– **i lage** ee <u>la</u>·yer	– marinated in brine
– **marineret** mah·<u>ree</u>·neh·rerdh	– marinated
salat sa·<u>lat</u>	salad
skinke <u>skin</u>·ger	ham
ål (i gelé/røget) owl (ee sheh·<u>leh</u>/<u>roi</u>·erdh)	(jellied/smoked) eel

Smørrebrød (open-faced sandwiches), comprised of buttered rye bread and sliced meat or cheese, have been a part of Danish cuisine for a long time; however, the fancier, more elaborate **smørrebrød** eaten on festive occasions appeared only in the late 1800s. Today **smørrebrød** is topped with a variety of delicacies: mounds of shrimp, eel, smoked salmon, marinated or smoked herring, liver paste, roast beef or pork and steak tartare. The sandwich is then garnished with a number of other ingredients: raw onions, cress, scrambled eggs, egg yolk, radishes, chives and pickled cucumbers to name a few.

Many large restaurants serve **smørrebrød**. You can select a traditional combination such as **dyrlægens natmad** (liver paté, corned beef and aspic **smørrebrød**), **rullepølse** (spiced meat roll) or **stjerneskud** (fish and shrimp **smørrebrød**), or you can name the individual items that you prefer.

With/Without…	**Med/Uden…** mehdh/<u>oo</u>·dhern…
I can't have…	**Jeg må ikke spise…** yie mow <u>ig</u>·ger <u>spee</u>·ser…

Vegetables

agurk a·<u>goork</u>	cucumber
artiskokker ah·tees·<u>koh</u>·kah	artichokes
asparges a·<u>spahs</u>	asparagus
aubergine oa·behr·<u>sheen</u>	eggplant [aubergine]
avocado a·vo·<u>ka</u>·doa	avocado
blomkål <u>blom</u>·kowl	cauliflower
…bønner …<u>bur</u>·nah	…beans
– **brune** <u>broo</u>·ner	– kidney
– **grønne** <u>grur</u>·ner	– green
– **hvide** <u>vee</u>·dher	– butter

I'd like…	**Jeg vil gerne have…** yie vil <u>gehr</u>·ner ha…
More…please.	**Mere…tak.** <u>meh</u>·ah…tahk

broccoli broh·koa·lee	broccoli
brøndkarse brurn·kah·ser	watercress
champignoner shahm·peen·yong·ah	mushrooms
courgette koor·sheh·ter	zucchini [courgette]
græskar grehs·kah	pumpkin
gulerødder goo·ler·rur·dhah	carrots
julesalat yoo·ler·sa·lat	endive [chickory]
kartofler ka·tohf·lah	potatoes
kastanjer ka·stan·yah	chestnuts
kål kowl	cabbage
løg loi	onions
majs mies	corn
peberfrugt peh·wah·froagt	peppers
porrer poa·rah	leeks
radiser rah·dee·sah	radishes
roer roa·ah	turnip
rosenkål roa·sern·kowl	Brussels sprouts
rødbeder rurdh·beh·dhah	beets [beetroot]
salat sa·lat	lettuce
selleri seh·ler·ree	celery
spinat spee·nat	spinach
søde kartofler sur·dher ka·tohf·lah	sweet potatoes
tomater toa·ma·dah	tomatoes
ærter ehr·dah	peas

With/Without…	**Med/Uden…** mehdh/oo·dhern…
I can't have…	**Jeg må ikke spise…** yie mow ig·ger spee·ser…

Spices and Staples

blandede urter <u>bla</u>·ner·dher <u>oor</u>·dah	mixed herbs
hvidløg <u>veedh</u>·loi	garlic
ingefær <u>ing</u>·er·fayr	ginger
kapers <u>ka</u>·pers	capers
linser <u>lin</u>·sah	lentils
mel mehl	flour
nudler <u>noodh</u>·lah	noodles
pasta <u>pa</u>·sta	pasta
peber <u>peh</u>·wah	pepper (spice)
peberrod <u>peh</u>·wah·roadh	horseradish
ris rees	rice
salt salt	salt
sennep <u>seh</u>·nerp	mustard
skalotteløg ska·<u>loh</u>·der·loi	shallot
spansk peber spansk <u>peh</u>·wah	pimiento pepper

Fruit and Nuts

abrikoser ah·bree·<u>koa</u>·sah	apricots
ananas <u>a</u>·na·nas	pineapple
appelsin ah·berl·<u>seen</u>	orange
banan ba·<u>nan</u>	banana
blommer <u>bloh</u>·mah	plums
blåbær <u>blaw</u>·behrr	blueberries
citron see·<u>troan</u>	lemon

I'd like…	**Jeg vil gerne have…** yie vil <u>gehr</u>·ner ha…
More…please.	**Mere…tak.** <u>meh</u>·ah…tahk

dadler <u>dadh</u>·lah	dates
fersken <u>fehrs</u>·gern	peach
figner <u>feey</u>·nah	figs
grapefrugt <u>grayb</u>·froagt	grapefruit
hasselnøddur <u>ha</u>·serl·nurdh·ah	hazelnuts
hindbær <u>hin</u>·behr	raspberries
jordbær <u>yoar</u>·behr	strawberries
jordnødder <u>yoar</u>·nurdh·ah	peanuts
kastanjer ka·<u>stan</u>·yah	chestnuts
kirsebær <u>keer</u>·ser·behr	cherries
lime liem	lime
mandarin man·da·<u>reen</u>	tangerine
mandler <u>man</u>·lah	almonds
melon meh·<u>loan</u>	melon
nektarin nehk·tah·<u>reen</u>	nectarine
pære <u>pay</u>·rah	pear
rabarber rah·<u>bah</u>·bah	rhubarb
rosiner roa·<u>see</u>·nah	raisins
solbær <u>soal</u>·behr	black currants
stikkelsbær <u>sti</u>·gerls·behr	gooseberries
tyttebær <u>tew</u>·der·behr	cranberries
valnødder <u>val</u>·nur·dha	walnuts
vandmelon <u>van</u>·meh·<u>loan</u>	watermelon
vindruer <u>veen</u>·droo·ah	grapes
æble <u>ay</u>·bler	apple

With/Without…	**Med/Uden…** mehdh/<u>oo</u>·dhern…
I can't have…	**Jeg må ikke spise…** yie mow <u>ig</u>·ger <u>spee</u>·ser…

Cheese

danablu <u>da</u>·na·bl**oo** — Danish blue cheese

danbo <u>dan</u>·boa — mild, firm cheese, sometimes with caraway seeds

elbo <u>ehl</u>·boa — hard cheese with a delicate taste

esrom <u>ehs</u>·roam — strong, slightly aromatic cheese

maribo <u>mah</u>·ree·boa — soft, mild cheese

molbo <u>mohl</u>·boa — rich and highly flavored

mycella mew·<u>seh</u>·la — similar to Danish blue cheese, but milder

samsø <u>sahm</u>·sur — mild, firm cheese with a sweet, nutty flavor

Dessert

appelsinfromage ah·berl·<u>seen</u>·froa·ma·sher — orange mousse

bondepige med slør <u>boa</u>·ner·pee·er mehdh slur — "veiled country maid": bread crumbs, apple sauce, cream, sugar

brune kager <u>broo</u>·ner <u>ka</u>·yah — spicy, crispy cookies [biscuits] with almond

citronfromage see·<u>troan</u>·froa·<u>ma</u>·sher — lemon mousse

flødekage <u>flur</u>·dher·<u>ka</u>·yer — cream cake

fromage froa·<u>ma</u>·sher — mousse

is ee**s** — ice cream

I'd like…	**Jeg vil gerne have…** yie vil <u>gehr</u>·ner ha…
More…please.	**Mere…tak.** <u>meh</u>·ah…tahk

kage <u>ka</u>·yer	cake
karamelrand kah·rah·<u>mehl</u>·rehn	caramel custard
pandekager <u>pa</u>·ner·<u>ka</u>·yah	thin pancakes
rødgrød med fløde <u>rurdh</u>·grurdh mehdh <u>flur</u>·dher	fruit jelly served with cream
små pandekager smow <u>pa</u>·ner·<u>ka</u>·yah	fritters
småkager <u>smaw</u>·ka·yer	cookies [biscuits]
æblekage med rasp og flødeskum <u>ay</u>·ble·<u>ka</u>·yer mehdh rahsp ow <u>flur</u>·dher·skoam	layers of stewed apple and cookie crumbs topped with whipped cream

Drinks

Essential

May I see the *wine list/drink menu*?	**Må jeg se *vinlisten/listen med drinks*?** mow yie seh <u>veen</u>·lis·tern/lis·tern mehdh drinks
What do you recommend?	**Hvad kan du anbefale?** vadh kan doo <u>an</u>·beh·<u>fa</u>·ler
I'd like a *bottle/glass* of *red/white* wine.	**Jeg vil gerne bede om en *flaske/et glas* *rødvin/hvidvin*.** yie vil <u>gehr</u>·ner beh ohm *ehn flas·ger/eht glas rurdh·veen/veedh·veen*
The house wine, please.	**Hustes vin, tak.** <u>hoo</u>·sets veen tahk
Another *bottle/glass*, please.	**En *flaske/Et glas* mere, tak.** ehn <u>flas</u>·ger/eht glas <u>meh</u>·ah tahk
I'd like a local beer.	**Jeg vil gerne bede om en lokal øl.** yie vil <u>gehr</u>·ner beh ohm ehn loa·<u>kal</u> url
Let me buy you a drink.	**Lad mig byde dig på en drink.** ladh mie <u>bew</u>·dher die paw ehn drink

Cheers!	**Skål!** skowl
A *coffee/tea*, please.	**En kop** *kaffe/te*, **tak.** ehn kohp *kah·fer/teh* tahk
With milk.	**Med mælk.** mehdh mehlk
With sugar.	**Med sukker.** mehdh <u>soa</u>·gah
With artificial sweetener.	**Med sødemiddel.** mehdh <u>sur</u>·dher·mee·dherl
...please.	**...tak.** ...tahk
– Juice	– **Juice** djoos
– Soda	– **Sodavand** <u>soa</u>·da·van
– *Sparkling/Still* water	– **Danskvand/Kildevand** <u>dansk</u>·van/<u>kee</u>·ler·van

Non-alcoholic Drinks

appelsinjuice ah·berl·<u>seen</u>·djoos	orange juice
grapefrugtjuice <u>grayb</u>·froagt·djoos	grapefruit juice
kaffe <u>kah</u>·fer	coffee
limonade li·moh·<u>na</u>·dher	lemonade
mineralvand mee·neh·<u>rahl</u>·van	mineral water
mælk mehlk	milk
te teh	tea
tomatjuice toa·<u>mat</u>·djoos	tomato juice
varm chokolade vahm shoa·koa·<u>la</u>·dher	hot chocolate
æblejuice <u>ay</u>·bler·djoos	apple juice

If you're not in the mood for Danish beer, there are a number of other drinks to enjoy. Strong filtered coffee is enjoyed throughout the day, even with meals. If you prefer tea, herbal tea is growing in popularity. **Varm chokolade** (hot chocolate) is often served to children, but is also enjoyed by adults. For a unique drink, you could try **hyldeblomstsaft** (elderflower juice), a delicacy that is making a comeback. Or, if you simply prefer water, try **danskvand** or **mineralvand** (sparking or mineral water) with a bit of citrus fruit.

Aperitifs, Cocktails and Liqueurs

akvavit ah·kva·<u>veet</u> — aquavit

aperitif ah·peh·ree·<u>teef</u> — aperitif

cognac <u>kon</u>·yahk — brandy

gin djin — gin

kalvados kal·va·<u>dohs</u> — apple brandy

kirsebærcognac <u>keer</u>·se·bayr·kon·yahk	cherry brandy
likør <u>lee</u>·kur	liquer
portvin <u>poart</u>·veen	port wine
rom rohm	rum
snaps snahps	schnapps
vermouth <u>vehr</u>·moot	vermouth
vodka vohd·ka	vodka
...whisky ...wis·keei	...whisky
– tør tur	– neat (straight)
– med isterninger mehdh <u>ees</u>·tehr·ning·ah	– on the rocks
– med lidt vand mehdh lit van	– with a little water
– med soda mehdh <u>soa</u>·da	– with soda water

Akvavit is a very popular drink in Denmark. Like vodka, it's distilled from potatoes, though barley is also used. The color varies according to the herbs and spices with which the drink is flavored.

Often served with a beer chaser, **akvavit** is drunk ice-cold, and makes an ideal accompaniment to Danish appetizers.

Beer

En flaske... ehn <u>flas</u>·ger...	A bottle of...
En pilsner, tak. ehn <u>pils</u>·nah tahk	A pilsner, please.
Et glas... eht glas...	A glass of...
– fadøl <u>fadh</u>·url	– draft [draught] beer
– udenlandsk øl <u>oo</u>·dhern·lansk url	– imported beer
– *lys/mørk øl* lews/murrk øl	– *light/dark* beer

i

The Carlsberg and Tuborg breweries are internationally known; however, Denmark has many microbreweries that offer a variety of refreshing beer options. If you feel like trying something new, taste one of the local brews.

A special event every year is **J-day**, whose name comes from the Danish word **Juleøl** (Christmas beer). **J-day** is normally celebrated the first Friday in November, when, at exactly 8:59 p.m., all the Danish breweries release their special, limited edition Christmas beer. Each company creates a new recipe each year. That evening you'll find pubs filled with people enjoying their first beer of the Christmas season. **Skål!** (Cheers!)

Wine

...vin ...veen	...wine
– hvid veedh	– white
– mousserende moo·<u>**seh**</u>·rern·der	– sparkling
– rosé roa·<u>seh</u>	– rosé
– rød rurdh	– red
– sød surdh	– sweet
– tør tur	– dry

Menu Reader

aborre <u>ah</u>·bohr	perch
abrikoser ah·bree·<u>koa</u>·sah	apricots
afkølet <u>ow</u>·kur·lerdh	chilled
agerhøne <u>a</u>·yer·hur·ner	roast partridge served with red currant jam or apple sauce and horseradish

agurk a·<u>goork</u>	cucumber
agurksalat a·<u>goork</u>·sa·lat	cucumber in vinegar dressing
ananas <u>a</u>·na·nas	pineapple
and an	duck
and, stegt an stehgt	roast duck stuffed with chestnuts or apples and prunes, served with olive or mushroom sauce
anisfrø <u>a</u>·nees·frur	aniseed
ansjoser an·<u>shoa</u>·sah	anchovies
aperitif ah·peh·ree·<u>teef</u>	aperitif
appelsin ah·berl·<u>seen</u>	orange
appelsinfromage ah·berl·<u>seen</u>·froa·ma·sher	orange mousse

appelsinmarmelade
ah·berl·<u>seen</u>·mah·mer·<u>la</u>·dher — marmalade

appelsinsovs ah·berl·<u>seen</u>·sows — orange sauce

artiskokker ah·tees·<u>koh</u>·gah — artichokes

asier <u>a</u>·shah — pickled gherkins

asparges a·<u>spahs</u> — asparagus

aspargeshoveder a·<u>spahs</u>·hoh·dhah — asparagus tips

aspargessuppe a·<u>spahs</u>·soa·per — asparagus soup

aubergine oa·ber·<u>sheen</u> — eggplant [aubergine]

avocado a·vo·<u>ka</u>·doa — avocado

bacon <u>bay</u>·kohn — bacon

banan ba·<u>nan</u> — banana

basilikum ba·<u>see</u>·lee·koam — basil

bearnaisesovs behr·<u>nays</u>·sows — a cream sauce flavored with tarragon and vinegar

beef <u>ohk</u>·ser·kurdh — oksekød

blandede grøntsager
<u>bla</u>·ner·dher <u>grun</u>·sa·yer — mixed vegetables

blandede urter bla·ner·dher <u>oor</u>·dah — mixed herbs

blandet hors d'oeuvre <u>bla</u>·nerdh ohr <u>durv</u>·rah — assorted appetizers

blodpølse <u>bloadh</u>·purl·sah — black pudding

blomkål <u>blohm</u>·kowl — cauliflower

blommer <u>bloh</u>·mah — plums

blå foreller blaw foa·<u>reh</u>·lah — poached trout, served with boiled potatoes, melted butter, horseradish and lemon

blåbær <u>blaw</u>·behr — blueberries

blåmuslinger <u>blaw</u>·moos·ling·ah	mussels
boller i karry <u>boh</u>·lah ee <u>kah</u>·ree	meatballs in a curry sauce
bondepige med slør <u>boh</u>·ner·pee·yer mehdh slur	"veiled country maid": a mixture of bread crumbs, apple sauce, cream and sugar
brisler <u>brees</u>·lah	sweetbreads
broccoli <u>broh</u>·koa·lee	broccoli
brun sovs broon sows	traditional thick gravy
brune kager <u>broo</u>·ner <u>ka</u>·yah	spicy, crisp cookies [biscuits] with almonds
brunede kartofler <u>broo</u>·ner·dher ka·<u>tohf</u>·lah	caramelized potatoes
brød brurdh	bread
brøndkarse <u>brurn</u>·<u>k</u>ah·ser	watercress
burger <u>bur</u>·gah	burger
bøftartar <u>burf</u>·tah·<u>tah</u>	beef tartare
bønner <u>bur</u>·nah	beans
champignoner <u>shahm</u>·peen·yohng·ah	mushrooms
champignonsuppe <u>sham</u>·peen·yohng·so·per	mushroom soup
chili <u>tjee</u>·lee	chili
(varm) chokolade (v<u>ah</u>m) shoa·koa·<u>la</u>·dher	(hot) chocolate
chokoladeis shoa·koa·<u>la</u>·dher·<u>ees</u>	chocolate ice cream
chutney-smør <u>tjoht</u>·nee smur	chutney butter
citron see·<u>troan</u>	lemon
citronfromage see·<u>troan</u>·froa·ma·sher	lemon mousse
citronmarinade see·<u>troan</u>·mah·ree·na·dher	marinade of lemon, oil, salt and pepper, paprika, herbs

citronsaft see·<u>troan</u>·sahft	lemon juice
cognac <u>kohn</u>·yahk	cognac
courgette koor·<u>sheh</u>·der	zucchini [courgette]
dadler <u>dadh</u>·lah	dates
danablu <u>da</u>·na·bloo	Danish blue cheese
danbo <u>dan</u>·boa	a mild, firm cheese, sometimes with caraway seeds
desserter deh·<u>sehr</u>·tah	desserts
dild deel	dill
drikkevarer <u>drig</u>·ger·vah·rah	beverages
due <u>doo</u>·er	pigeon
dyrekød <u>dew</u>·rer·kurdh	venison
dyreryg <u>dew</u>·rer·rurg	saddle (cut of meat)
eddike <u>eh</u>·dhee·ker	vinegar
elbo <u>ehl</u>·boa	a hard cheese with a delicate taste
engelsk bøf <u>ehng</u>·erlsk burf	fillet of beef with onions and boiled potatoes
esrom <u>ehs</u>·roam	a strong, slightly aromatic cheese of spongy texture
estragon eh·strah·<u>gong</u>	tarragon
fadøl <u>fadh</u>·url	draft [draught] beer
fasan fa·<u>san</u>	pheasant
fennikel <u>feh</u>·nee·kerl	fennel
fersken <u>fehrs</u>·gern	peach
figner <u>feey</u>·nah	figs

fisk fisk	fish
fjerkræ <u>fyehr</u>·kray	poultry
flaskeøl <u>flas</u>·ger·url	bottled beer
flæskesteg med svær <u>flay</u>·sger·stie mehdh svehr	roast pork with crackling
flødekage <u>flur</u>·dher·ka·yer	cream cake
flødepeberrod <u>flur</u>·dher·<u>peh</u>·wah·roadh	horseradish cream dressing
forel foa·<u>rehl</u>	trout
forloren skildpadde foh·<u>loh</u>·rern <u>skil</u>·pa·dher	"mock turtle": a very traditional Danish dish consisting of meat, meatballs and fish balls
franskbrød <u>frahnsk</u>·brurdh	white bread
frikadeller fri·ka·<u>dehl</u>·lah	meatballs
fromage froa·<u>ma</u>·sher	mousse
frugt froagt	fruit
frugtsuppe <u>froagt</u>·soa·per	fruit soup, composed of a variety of dried fruits, served chilled or hot
fuldkornsbrød <u>fool</u>·koarns·brurdh	whole-grain bread
fyldte tomater <u>fewl</u>·der toh·<u>ma</u>·dah	stuffed tomatoes
fårekød <u>faw</u>·er·kurdh	mutton
gedde <u>geh</u>·dher	pike
gin djin	gin
grapefrugt <u>grayb</u>·froagt	grapefruit
grillstegt kylling <u>greel</u>·stehgt <u>kew</u>·ling	barbecued chicken
grisehoved <u>gree</u>·ser·ho·wedh	pig's head

grisetæer gree·ser·tehr	pig's feet
grydedesteg grew·dher·stie	pot roast
græskar grehs·kah	pumpkin
grønne bønner grurn·ner bur·nah	green beans
grøntsager grurn·sa·yah	vegetables
gule ærter goo·ler ehr·dah	split-pea soup with salt pork
gulerødder goo·ler·rur·dhah	carrots
gås gows	goose
gåselever gow·ser·leh·wah	goose liver
hakkebøf hah·ger·burf	beef patties
hamburgerryg hahm·boh·rurg	smoked, salted saddle of pork, roasted and served in thin slices with Cumberland (cucumber-based) sauce
hare har·rer	hare
hasselnødder ha·serl·nur·dhah	hazelnuts
havregrød how·er·grurdh	porridge
helleflynder heh·ler·flew·nah	halibut
hindbær hin·behr	raspberries
honning hoh·ning	honey
hummer hoa·mah	lobster
hummersuppe hoa·mah·soa·per	lobster chowder
hvidløg veedh·loi	garlic
hvidvinssovs veedh·veens·sows	white wine sauce
hønsekødsuppe hurn·ser·kurdhs·soa·per	chicken and vegetable soup

hårdkogt <u>haw</u>·kohgtt	hard-boiled
ingefær <u>ing</u>·er·fehr	ginger
is <u>ee</u>s	ice cream
italiensk salat ee·tal·<u>yehn</u>sk sa·<u>lat</u>	diced carrots and asparagus, green peas and mayonnaise
jordbær <u>yoar</u>·behr	strawberries
jordbæris <u>yoar</u>·behr·<u>ee</u>s	strawberry ice cream
jordnødder <u>yoar</u>·nur·dhah	peanuts
juice djoos	juice
julesalat <u>yoo</u>·ler·sa·<u>lat</u>	endive
kaffe kah·<u>fer</u>	coffee
kaffeinfri kah·feh·<u>een</u>·free	decaffeinated
kage <u>ka</u>·yer	cake
kalkun kal·<u>koon</u>	turkey
kalkunragout kal·<u>koon</u> rah·<u>goo</u>	turkey in a sweet-and-sour gravy, served with mashed potatoes or a chestnut purée
kalvebrissel <u>kal</u>·ver·bris·serl	calf's sweetbread
kalvekød kal·ver·kurdh	veal
kanel ka·<u>nehl</u>	cinnamon
kanin ka·<u>neen</u>	rabbit
kanin i flødepeberrod ka·<u>neen</u> ee <u>flur</u>·dher·peh·wah·roadh	rabbit stew with horseradish cream dressing, roast mushroom and onions
kapers <u>ka</u>·pahs	capers
karaffel ka·<u>rah</u>·ferl	carafe

karamelrand kah·rah·<u>mehl</u>·ran — caramel custard

karpe <u>kah</u>·per — carp

kartoffel croquettes ka·<u>toh</u>·ferl kroa·<u>keh</u>·dah — potato croquettes

kartoffelmos (med æbler) ka·<u>toh</u>·ferl·moas (mehdh **ay-b**lah) — mashed potatoes (with apple purée)

kartoffelsalat ka·toh·ferl·sa·<u>lat</u> — potato salad

kartofler ka·<u>tohf</u>·lah — potatoes

kastaniesovs ka·<u>stan</u>·yer·sows — chestnut sauce

kastanjer ka·<u>stan</u>·yah — chestnuts

kaviar <u>ka</u>·vee·ah — caviar

kirsebær <u>keer</u>·ser·behr — cherries

kirsebærcognac keer·se·bayr·<u>kohn</u>·yahk — cherry brandy

klar suppe med boller og grønsager klah <u>soa</u>·**per** mehdh <u>boh</u>·lah ow <u>grurn</u>·sa·yah — vegetable soup with meatballs

kokosnød <u>koa</u>·kohs·nurdh — coconut

koldt bord kohlt boar — smorgasbord

koldt kødpålæg kolt <u>kurdh</u>·paw·laygh — cold cuts

kommen <u>koh</u>·mern — cumin

kotelet koa·der·<u>leht</u> — chop, cutlet

krebs krehbs — crab

kryddernellike <u>krew</u>·dher·neh·lee·ker — clove

kråsesuppe <u>krow</u>·ser·soa·per — a sweet-sour chicken giblets soup, often with dried apples

kvæde <u>kvay</u>·dher — quince

kylling <u>kew</u>·ling — chicken

kylling med rejer og asparges kew·ling mehdh rie·ah ow a·spahs	chicken in an asparagus sauce and garnished with shrimp
kyllingesalat kew·ling·er·sa·lat	chicken, macaroni, tomato, peppers, olives, peas, lettuce and mushrooms, covered with a tomato dressing
kød kurdh	meat
kødboller kurdh·boh·lah	meatballs
labskovs lahb·skows	beef, diced potatoes, slices of carrots and onions, served with rye bread
lagkage lahw·ka·yer	layer cake
laks lahks	salmon
lam lahm	lamb
laurbærblad lah·wer·behr·bla·dher	bay leaf
lever leh·wah	liver
likør lee·kur	liqueur
lime liem	lime
limonade li·moa·na·dher	lemonade
linser lin·sah	lentils
lys hvidtøl lews veed·url	a pale, sweetish, low-alcohol beer
løg loi	onions
løgsovs loi·sows	onion sauce
majroer mie·roa·ah	turnips
majs mies	corn

makrel ma·<u>krehl</u>	mackerel
makrelsalat ma·<u>krehl</u>·sa·<u>lat</u>	mackerel in tomato sauce topped with mayonnaise
maltøl <u>malt</u>·url	a very heavy beer, regarded as a tonic
mandarin man·da·<u>reen</u>	tangerine
mandelgræskar <u>ma</u>·nerl·grehs·kar	vegetable marrow
mandler <u>man</u>·lah	almonds
maribo <u>mah</u>·ree·boa	a soft, mild cheese
marineret mah·ree·<u>neh</u>·rerdh	marinated
medisterpølse meh·<u>dees</u>·dah·purl·sah	spiced pork sausage, served with stewed vegetables or sautéed cabbage and potatoes
medium <u>meh</u>·dee·oam	medium
mel mehl	flour
melon meh·<u>loan</u>	melon
merian <u>meh</u>·ree·an	marjoram
milkshake <u>meelk</u>·sjayk	milkshake
mineralvand mee·mer·<u>rahl</u>·van	mineral water
molbo <u>mol</u>·boa	like Edam; a rich and highly flavored cheese
mousserende moo·<u>seh</u>·rern·der	sparkling (wine)
muskatnød moo·<u>skat</u>·nurdh	nutmeg
muslinger <u>moos</u>·ling·ah	mussels
mycella mew·<u>sehl</u>·la	similar to Danish blue cheese, but milder
mynte <u>mewn</u>·der	mint
mælk mehlk	milk

mørkt hvidtøl murkt <u>veed</u>·url	a dark beer; sweet and creamy
nektarin nehk·tah·<u>reen</u>	nectarine
nudler <u>noodh</u>·lah	noodles
nye kartofler <u>new</u>·er ka·<u>tohf</u>·lah	new potatoes
nyrer <u>new</u>·rah	kidneys
oksefilet <u>ohk</u>·ser·fee·leh	fillet
oksehale <u>ohk</u>·ser·ha·ler	oxtail
oksemørbrad <u>ohk</u>·ser·mur·brahdh	tenderloin
oksesteg <u>ohk</u>·ser·stie	roast beef
oksetyndsteg <u>ohk</u>·ser·turn·stie	sirloin
oliven (fyldte) oa·<u>lee</u>·vern (<u>fewl</u>·der)	olives (stuffed)
omelet oa·mer·<u>leht</u>	omelet
oregano oh·reh·<u>ga</u>·noa	oregano
ost oast	cheese
ovnstegt <u>own</u>·stehght	roast
pandekager <u>pa</u>·ner·ka·yah	pancakes
paprika <u>pahp</u>·ree·ka	paprika
pasta <u>pa</u>·sta	pasta
pattegris <u>pah</u>·der·grees	suckling pig
peber <u>peh</u>·wah	pepper (spice)
peberfrugt <u>peh</u>·wah·froagt	pepper (vegetable)
peberrod <u>peh</u>·wah·<u>roadh</u>	horseradish
perlehøne <u>pehr</u>·ler·<u>hur</u>·ner	guinea fowl
persille pehr·<u>see</u>·ler	parsley
persillesovs pehr·<u>see</u>·ler·sows	parsley sauce
pighvar <u>peeg</u>·vah	turbot

pocheret æg poa-<u>sheh</u>-rerdh ayg	poached eggs
pommes frites pohm freet	French fries [chips]
porrer <u>poa</u>-ah	leeks
portvin <u>poart</u>-veen	port wine
pumpernikkel-brød <u>pohm</u>-bah-ni-ker-brurdh	pumpernickel bread
purløg <u>poor</u>-loi	chives
pære <u>pay</u>-ah	pear
pølse <u>purl</u>-ser	sausage
rabarber rah-<u>bah</u>-bah	rhubarb
radiser rah-<u>dee</u>-sah	radishes
ragout ra-<u>goo</u>	stew
rejer <u>rie</u>-ah	shrimp [prawns]
remoulade reh-moa-<u>la</u>-dher	mustard and herb cream dressing
rensdyr <u>rehns</u>-dewr	reindeer
ribbenssteg <u>ree</u>-behns-stie	ribsteak
rice rees	rice
ristet brød <u>ris</u>-terdh brurdh	toast
roer <u>roa</u>-ah	turnips
rogn rown	roe
rollmops <u>rol</u>-mohps	pickled herring [rollmops]
rom rohm	rum
rosé roa-<u>seh</u>	rosé
rosemarin roas-mah-<u>reen</u>	rosemary
rosenkål <u>roa</u>-sern-kowl	Brussels sprouts
rosiner roa-<u>see</u>-nah	raisins

rugbrød <u>roo</u>·brurdh	rye bread
rundstykker <u>roan</u>·stur·gah	rolls
rype <u>rew</u>·per	grouse
røget sild <u>roi</u>·erdh seel	smoked herring
røræg <u>rur</u>·ayg	scrambled eggs
rørt smør rurt smur	flavored cream butter
safran <u>sa</u>·fran	saffron
salat sa·<u>lat</u>	salad; lettuce
salt salt	salt
saltagurk <u>salt</u>·a·goork	pickles
saltkød <u>salt</u>·kurdh	salt beef slices
salvie sal·<u>vee</u>·er	sage
samsø <u>sahm</u>·sur	a mild, firm cheese with a sweet, nutty flavor
sardiner sah·<u>dee</u>·nah	sardines
selleri <u>seh</u>·leh·ree	celery
sellerisalat <u>seh</u>·leh·ree·sa·<u>lat</u>	celery salad with a cheese dressing or mayonnaise
sellerisovs <u>seh</u>·leh·ree·sows	celery-flavored sauce with sherry
sennep <u>seh</u>·nerp	mustard
sennepssovs <u>seh</u>·nerps·sows	mustard sauce
sild seel	herring
sild i karry seel ee <u>kah</u>·ree	herring in curry sauce
sild med løg seel mehdh loi	herring with onion

sild, røget seel <u>roi</u>·erdh — herring, smoked, on dark rye bread, garnished with a raw egg yolk, radishes and chives

sildesalat <u>see</u>·ler·sa·<u>lat</u> — marinated or pickled herring, beet, apple and pickles in a spicy dressing

skaldyr <u>skal</u>·dewr — seafood

skalotteløg ska·<u>loh</u>·ter·loi — shallot

skank skahnk — shank

skibsøl <u>skeebs</u>·url — dark "ship's beer" noted for its smoked-malt character

skidne æg <u>skeedh</u>·ner ayg — poached or hard-boiled eggs in a cream sauce, with fish and mustard

skinke <u>skin</u>·ger — ham

skinke og æg <u>skin</u>·ger ow ayg — ham and eggs

skrubbe <u>skroa</u>·ber — flounder

smør smur — butter

smørrebrød <u>smur</u>·er·brurdh — famous Danish open-faced sandwich

små pandekager smow <u>pa</u>·ner·**ka**·yah — fritters

småkager <u>smow</u>·**ka**·yah — cookies [biscuits]

solbær <u>soal</u>·behr — black currants

spansk peber spansk <u>peh</u>·wah — pimiento pepper

spegepølse <u>spie</u>·er·purl·ser — salami

spejlæg <u>spiel</u>·ayg — fried eggs

spinat spee·<u>nat</u>	spinach
spiseolie <u>spee</u>·ser·oal·yer	oil
sprængt oksebryst sprayngt <u>ohk</u>·ser·brurst	boiled, salted beef brisket
spækket steg <u>speh</u>·gerdh stie	larded roast
stærk salatsovs stehrk sa·<u>lat</u>·sows	egg yolks, vinegar or lemon juice, oil, salt and pepper or paprika, Worcester sauce, onion or garlic and dill, all mixed with whipped cream
stegte kartofler <u>stehg</u>·der ka·<u>tohf</u>·lah	sautéed potatoes
stikkelsbær <u>sti</u>·kerls·behr	gooseberries
store rejer stoa·ah <u>rie</u>·ah	shrimp [prawns]
stør stur	sturgeon
sukker <u>soa</u>·gah	sugar
suppe <u>soa</u>·pah	soup
sylteagurker <u>sewl</u>·der·a·goor·kah	gherkins
syltetøj <u>sewl</u>·der·toi	jam
søde kartofler <u>sur</u>·dher ka·<u>tohf</u>·lah	sweet potatoes
sødemiddel <u>sur</u>·dher·mee·dherl	artificial sweetener
søtunge <u>sur</u>·toang·ah	sole
torsk <u>toh</u>sk	cod
torsk, kogt <u>toh</u>sk kohgt	cod, poached
torskerogn, ristet <u>toh</u>s·ger·rown <u>ris</u>·terdh	cod roe, fried
tunfisk <u>toon</u>·fisk	tuna
tunge <u>toang</u>·er	tongue
tyttebær <u>tew</u>·der·behr	cranberries

tørret frugt <u>tur</u>·erdh froagt	dried fruit
ung and oang an	duckling
vagtel <u>vahg</u>·derl	quail
valnødder <u>val</u>·nur·dhah	walnuts
vand van	water
vandmelon <u>van</u>·meh·<u>loan</u>	watermelon
vanilje va·<u>nil</u>·yer	vanilla
vegetar veh·ger·<u>tah</u>	vegetarian
vermouth <u>vehr</u>·moot	vermouth
vildsvin <u>veel</u>·sveen	wild boar
vildt veelt	game
vildtsovs <u>veelt</u>·sows	sauce of fresh cream and red currant jam
vin veen	wine
vinaigrette-sovs vee·na·<u>greht</u>·sows	vinegar and oil dressing
vindruer <u>veen</u>·droo·ah	grapes
vinkogt laks med pikant sovs <u>veen</u>·kogt lahks mehdh pee·<u>kant</u> sows	salmon poached in white wine, dressed with a spicy sauce
vodka <u>vohd</u>·ka	vodka
whisky <u>whis</u>·kee	whisky
ymersovs <u>ew</u>·mah·sows	lemon juice, spices and herbs, mixed with milk or cream
yoghurt <u>yoo</u>·goord	yogurt
æble <u>ay</u>·bler	apple
æbleflæsk <u>ay</u>·bler·flaysk	smoked bacon with onions and sautéed apple rings

æblekage med rasp og fløadeskum stewed apples with
<u>ay</u>·bler·**ka**·yer mehdh rahsp vanilla served with
ow fl<u>ur</u>·dher·skoam layers of cookie
crumbs and topped
with whipped cream

æblesuppe ay·bler·soa·per apple soup

æg ayg egg

æggekage <u>ay</u>·ger·**ka**·yer scrambled eggs
with onions, chives,
potatoes and bacon

æggesovs <u>ay</u>·ger·sows egg sauce

æggeretter <u>ay</u>·ger·reh·dah egg dishes

ægte skildpaddesuppe turtle soup
ehg·der <u>skil</u>·**pa**·dher·soa·per

øl url beer

øllebrød <u>ur</u>·lah·brurdh rye bread cooked with
Danish beer, sugar
and lemon, served
with milk and cream

ørred <u>ur</u>·rerdh trout

østers <u>urs</u>·dahs oysters

ål owl eel

ål, stegt med stuvede kartofler owl stehgt eel, fried, with diced
mehdh <u>stoo</u>·ver·dher ka·<u>tof</u>·lah potatoes in a white
sauce

ålesuppe <u>ow</u>·ler·soa·per sweet-and-sour eel
soup, with apples and
prunes, served with
dark rye bread

▼ *People*

Talking

Essential

Hello!	**Hej!** hie
How are you?	**Hvordan har du det?** voar·<u>dan</u> har doo deh
Fine, thanks.	**Godt, tak.** goht tahk
Excuse me!	**Undskyld!** <u>oan</u>·skewl
Do you speak English?	**Kan du tale engelsk?** kan doo <u>ta</u>·ler <u>ehng</u>·erlsk
What's your name?	**Hvad hedder du?** vadh <u>heh</u>·dhah doo
My name is…	**Mit navn er…** meet nown ehr…
Nice to meet you.	**Det glæder mig at træffe dig.** deh <u>glay</u>·dhah mie ad <u>treh</u>·fer die
Where are you from?	**Hvor kommer du fra?** voar <u>koh</u>·mah doo frah
I'm from *the U.S./the U.K.*	**Jeg kommer fra *USA/England.*** yie <u>koh</u>·mah frah *oo·ehs·<u>a</u>/<u>ehng</u>·lan*
What do you do?	**Hvad laver du?** vadh <u>la</u>·vah doo
I work for…	**Jeg arbejder hos…** yie **<u>ah</u>**·bey·dah hohs…
I'm a student.	**Jeg studerer.** yie stoo·<u>deh</u>·rah
I'm retired.	**Jeg er pensionist.** yie ehr pang·shoa·<u>neest</u>
Do you like…?	**Kan du lide…?** kan doo lee…
Goodbye.	**Farvel.** fah·<u>vehl</u>
See you later.	**På gensyn.** paw <u>gehn</u>·sewn

De (the formal form of you) is generally no longer used to address strangers, but is restricted to formal letters, addressing the elderly or addressing members of the royal family. As a general rule, **du** can be used in all situations without offending anyone.

Communication Difficulties

Do you speak English?	**Kan du tale engelsk?** kan doo <u>ta</u>·ler <u>ehng</u>·erlsk
Does anyone here speak English?	**Er der nogen her, der kan tale engelsk?** ehr dehr <u>noa</u>·ern hehr dehr kan <u>ta</u>·ler <u>ehng</u>·erlsk
I don't speak (much) Danish.	**Jeg kan ikke tale (ret meget) dansk.** yie kan <u>ig</u>·ger <u>ta</u>·ler (reht <u>mie</u>·erdh) dansk
Can you speak more slowly?	**Kan du tale lidt langsommere?** kan doo <u>ta</u>·ler lit <u>lang</u>·sohm·ah
Can you repeat that?	**Kan du gentage det?** kan doo <u>gehn</u>·**ta**·yer deh
What was that?	**Hvad var det?** vadh vah deh
Please write it down.	**Vær rar og skriv det ned.** vehr rah ow skreew deh nedh
Can you translate this for me?	**Kan du oversætte det her for mig?** kan doo <u>oh</u>·wah·seh·der deh hehr for mie
What does this mean?	**Hvad betyder det her?** vadh beh·<u>tew</u>·dhah deh hehr
I understand.	**Jeg forstår det godt.** yie foh·<u>staw</u> deh goht
I don't understand.	**Jeg forstår det ikke.** yie foh·<u>staw</u> deh <u>ig</u>·ger
Do you understand?	**Kan du forstå det?** kan doo foh·<u>staw</u> deh

You May Hear...

Jeg taler kun lidt engelsk. yie <u>ta</u>·lah koon lit <u>ehng</u>·erlsk	I only speak a little English.
Jeg kan ikke tale engelsk. yie kan <u>ig</u>·ger <u>ta</u>·ler <u>ehng</u>·erlsk	I don't speak English.

Making Friends

Hello!	**Hej!** hie
Good morning.	**God morgen.** goadh·<u>mohn</u>
Good afternoon.	**God eftermiddag.** goadh·<u>ef</u>·tah·mi·da
Good evening.	**God aften.** goadh·<u>ahf</u>·tern
My name is…	**Mit navn er…** meet nown ehr…
What's your name?	**Hvad hedder du?** vadh <u>heh</u>·dhah doo
Let me introduce you to…	**Lad mig præsentere dig for…** ladh mie pray·sehn·<u>teh</u>·rer die foh…
Nice to meet you.	**Det glæder mig at træffe dig.** deh <u>glay</u>·dhah mie ad <u>tray</u>·fer die
How are you?	**Hvordan har du det?** voar·<u>dan</u> hah doo deh
Fine, thanks.	**Godt, tak.** goht tahk
And you?	**Og hvordan har du det?** ow voar·<u>dan</u> hah doo deh

> *i* In Denmark, upon meeting, it is customary to shake hands for both men and women. Close friends (male-female/female-female) may give kisses on the cheeks. As a greeting, you could say **Går det godt?** (How's it going?) or **Hva så?** (What's up?). **Hej** (general greeting) in Danish is used both for hello or hi and bye.

Travel Talk

I'm here…	**Jeg er her…** yie ehr hehr…
– on business	**– på forretningsrejse** pow foh·<u>reht</u>·nings·rie·ser
– on vacation [holiday]	**– på ferie** paw <u>fehr</u>·yer
– studying	**– for at studere** foh ad stoo·<u>deh</u>·er
I'm staying for…	**Jeg skal være her…** yie skal <u>vay</u>·ah hehr…
I've been here…	**Jeg har været her…** yie hah <u>vay</u>·erdh hehr…
– a day	**– en dag** ehn da
– a week	**– en uge** ehn <u>oo</u>·er
– a month	**– en måned** ehn <u>mow</u>·nerdh

▶ For numbers, see page 162.

Where are you from?	**Hvor kommer du fra?** voar <u>koh</u>·mah doo frah
I'm from…	**Jeg kommer fra…** yie <u>koh</u>·mah frah…

Relationships

Who are you with?	**Hvem er du her sammen med?** vehm ehr doo hehr <u>sah</u>·mern mehdh
I'm on my own.	**Jeg er her alene.** yie ehr hehr a·<u>leh</u>·ner
I'm with…	**Jeg er her sammen med…** yie ehr hehr <u>sah</u>·mern mehdh…
– my *husband/wife*	**– min *mand/kone*** meen man/<u>koa</u>·ner
– my *boyfriend/ girlfriend*	**– min kæreste** meen <u>kehr</u>·sder
– a friend	**– en ven** ehn vehn
– a colleague	**– en kollega** ehn koa·<u>leh</u>·ga
When's your birthday?	**Hvornår et det din fødselsdag?** voar·<u>naw</u> ehr deh d**ee**n <u>fur</u>·sehls·da

| How old are you? | **Hvor gammel er du?** voar <u>gah</u>·merl ehr doo |
| I'm... | **Jeg er...** yie ehr... |

▶For numbers, see page 162.

Are you married?	**Er du gift?** ehr doo geefd
I'm...	**Jeg er...** yie ehr...
– single	**– ugift** <u>oo</u>·geefd
– in a relationship	**– i et seriøst forhold** ee eht seh·ree·<u>ursd</u> <u>foh</u>·hohl
– married	**– gift** geefd
– divorced	**– skilt** skild
– separated	**– separeret** seh·pah·<u>reh</u>·erdh
I'm widowed.	**Jeg er enkemand**♂/**enke**♀. yie ehr <u>ehn</u>·ker·man ♂/<u>ehn</u>·ker ♀
Do you have *children/ grandchildren*?	**Har du nogen *børn/børnebørn*?** hah doo noa·ern *burn/<u>bur</u>·ner·burn*

Work and School

What do you do?	**Hvad laver du?** vadh <u>la</u>·ver doo
What are you studying?	**Hvad studerer du?** vadh stoo·<u>deh</u>·ah doo
I'm studying...	**Jeg studerer...** yie stoo·<u>deh</u>·ah...
I work *full time/part time*.	**Jeg arbejder *fuldtids/deltids*.** yie <u>ah</u>·bey·dah *<u>fool</u>·teedhs/<u>dehl</u>·teedhs*
I work at home.	**Jeg arbejder hjemmefra.** yie <u>ah</u>·bey·dah <u>yeh</u>·mer·frah
Who do you work for?	**Hvor arbejder du henne?** voar <u>ah</u>·bey·dah doo <u>heh</u>·ner

| I work for… | **Jeg arbejder hos…** yie **ah**·bey·dah hohs… |
| Here's my business card. | **Her er mit visitkort.** hehr ehr meet vee·<u>seet</u>·kawd |

▶For business travel, see page 139.

Weather

What's the weather forecast?	**Hvordan er vejrudsigten?** voar·<u>dan</u> ehr <u>vehr</u>·oodh·sig·dern
What *beautiful/terrible* weather!	**Hvor er det *smukt/frygteligt* vejr!** voar ehr deh *smoagt/<u>frurg</u>·ter·leed* vayr
It's…	**Det…** deh…
– cool	**– er koldt** ehr kohlt
– icy	**– er iskoldt** ehr <u>ees</u>·kohlt
– rainy	**– regner** <u>rie</u>·nah
– snowy	**– sner** snehr
– warm	**– er varmt** ehr vahmt
It's sunny.	**Solen skinner.** <u>soa</u>·lern <u>ski</u>·nah
Do I need *a jacket/ an umbrella*?	**Har jeg brug for en *jakke/paraply*?** hah yie broo foh ehn *<u>yah</u>·ker/pah·rah·<u>plew</u>*

▶For temperature, see page 167.

Romance

Essential

| Would you like to go out for a *drink/meal*? | **Har du lyst til at gå ud og få *en drink/ noget at spise*?** hah doo lurst til ad gow ood ow fow *ehn drink/<u>noa</u>·erdh ad <u>spee</u>·ser* |
| What are your plans for *tonight/tomorrow*? | **Hvad er dine planer for *i aften/i morgen*?** vadh ehr <u>dee</u>·ner <u>pla</u>·nah foh *ee <u>ahf</u>·tern/ee <u>mohn</u>* |

Can I have your number?	**Må jeg få dit nummer?** mow yie fow deet <u>noa</u>·mah
Can I join you?	**Må jeg komme med dig?** mow yie <u>koh</u>·mer mehdh die
Let me buy you a drink.	**Lad mig købe dig en drink.** ladh mie <u>kur</u>·ber die ehn drink
I like you.	**Jeg kan lide dig.** yie kan lee die
I love you.	**Jeg elsker dig.** yie <u>ehl</u>·skah die

Making Plans

What are your plans for…?	**Hvad er dine planer for…?** vadh ehr <u>dee</u>·ner <u>pla</u>·nah foh…
– tonight	**– i aften** ee <u>ahf</u>·tern
– tomorrow	**– i morgen** ee mohn
– this weekend	**– weekenden** <u>vee</u>·gehn·dern
Where would you like to go?	**Hvor har du lyst til at gå hen?** voar hah doo lurst til ad gow hehn
I'd like to go to…	**Jeg vil gerne…** yie vil <u>gehr</u>·ner…
Do you like…?	**Har du lyst til at…?** hah doo lurst til ad…
Can I have your number/e-mail?	**Må jeg få *dit nummer/din e-mail adresse*?** mow yie fow deet <u>noa</u>·mah/deen <u>ee</u>·mayl·a·drah·ser

▶ For e-mail and phone, see page 46.

Pick-up [Chat-up] Lines

Can I join you?	**Må jeg komme med dig?** mow yie <u>koh</u>·mer mehdh die
You're very attractive.	**Du er meget køn.** doo ehr <u>mie</u>·erdh kurn
Shall we go somewhere quieter?	**Skal vi gå hen et sted, hvor der er mere stille?** skal vee gow hen eht stehdh voar dehr ehr <u>meh</u>·ah sti·ler

Accepting and Rejecting ——————

Thanks, I'd love to.	**Tak, det vil jeg meget gerne.** tahk deh vil yie <u>mie</u>·erdh <u>gehr</u>·ner
Where can we meet?	**Hvor skal vi mødes?** voar skal vee <u>mur</u>·dhers
I'll meet you at *the bar/your hotel.*	**Jeg møder dig *i baren/på dit hotel.*** yie <u>mur</u>·dhah die *ee <u>bah</u>n/paw deet hoa·<u>tehl</u>*
I'll come by at…	**Jeg kommer klokken…** yie <u>koh</u>·mah kloh·gehrn…
What's your address?	**Hvad er din adresse?** vadh ehr deen a·<u>drah</u>·ser
Thank you, but I'm busy.	**Tak, men jeg er desværre optaget.** tahk mehn yie ehr deh·<u>svehr</u> ohp·ta·erdh
No thanks, I'm not interested.	**Nej tak, jeg er ikke interesseret.** nie tahk yie ehr ig·ger in·trah·<u>seh</u>·erdh

| Leave me alone! | **Vær rar og lad mig være i fred!** vehr rah ow la mie <u>vay</u>·er ee frehdh |
| Stop bothering me! | **Lad mig være i fred!** la mie <u>vay</u>·er ee frehdh |

Getting Physical

Can I *hug/kiss* you?	**Må jeg *kramme/kysse* dig?** mow yie *krah·mer/<u>kur</u>·ser* die
Yes.	**Ja.** ya
No.	**Nej.** nie
Stop!	**Stop!** stohb

Sexual Preferences

Are you gay?	**Er du homoseksuel?** ehr doo <u>hoa</u>·moa·sehk·soo·ehl
I'm...	**Jeg er...** yie ehr...
– heterosexual	– **heteroseksuel** <u>heh</u>·teh·roa·sehk·soo·ehl
– homosexual	– **homoseksuel** <u>hoa</u>·moa·sehk·soo·ehl
– bisexual	– **biseksuel** <u>bee</u>·sehk·soo·ehl

▼ Fun

Sightseeing

Essential

Where's the tourist information office?	**Hvor ligger turistinformationen?** voar li·gah too·reest·in·foh·ma·sho**a**·nern
What are the main points of interest?	**Hvad er de vigtigste seværdigheder?** vadh ehr dee vig·tee·ster seh·vehr·dee·heh·dhah
Do you offer tours in English?	**Tilbyder I turer på engelsk?** til·bew·dhah ee too·ah paw ehng·erlsk
Can I have a *map/ guide*?	**Må jeg få *et kort/en guidebog*?** mow yie fow *eht kawd/ehn guide·bow*

Tourist Information Office

Do you have any information on...?	**Har du nogen information om...?** hah doo n**oa**·ern in·foh·ma·sh**oan** ohm...
Can you recommend...?	**Kan du anbefale...?** kan doo an·beh·fa·ler...
– a boat trip	– **en bådtur** ehn bowdh·toor
– an excursion	– **en udflugt** ehn oodh·floagt
– a sightseeing tour	– **en rundtur** ehn roan·toor

Tours

I'd like to go on the tour to…	**Jeg vil gerne på turen til…** yie vil <u>gehr</u>·ner paw <u>too</u>·ern til…
When's the next tour?	**Hvornår starter den næste tur?** voar·<u>naw</u> star·dah dehn nehs·der toor
Are there tours in English?	**Er der ture på engelsk?** ehr dehr <u>too</u>·ah paw ehng·erlsk
Is there an English-speaking *guide/audio guide*?	**Er der en engelsktalende *guide/engelsk lydguide*?** ehr dehr ehn <u>ehng</u>·erlsk·<u>ta</u>·ler·ner guide/<u>ehng</u>·erlsk <u>lewdh</u>·guide
What time do we *leave/return*?	**Hvad tid *tager vi afsted/kommer vi tilbage*?** vadh teedh tah vee a·<u>stehdh</u>/<u>koh</u>·mah vee til·<u>ba</u>·yer
We'd like to see…	**Vi vil gerne se…** vee vil <u>gehr</u>·ner seh…
Can we stop here…?	**Kan vi stoppe her…?** kan vee <u>stoh</u>·ber hehr…
– to take photographs	**– for at tage billeder** foh ad ta <u>bil</u>·ler·dhah
– to buy souvenirs	**– for at købe souvenirs** foh ad <u>kur</u>·ber <u>sou</u>·ve·neers
– to use the restroom [toilet]	**– for at gå på toilettet** foh ad gow paw toa·ee·<u>leh</u>·derdh
Is there access for the disabled?	**Er der adgang for handicappede?** ehr dehr <u>adh</u>·gahng foh <u>han</u>·dee·kah·per·dher

▶For ticketing, see page 21.

Tourist information offices are located throughout Denmark. The local tourist office can provide a wealth of information on accommodation, activities and other entertainment. An extensive list of all the tourist offices in Denmark can be found on Visit Denmark, the Danish Tourist Board's website.

▶For useful websites, see page 168.

Sights

Where *is/are*...?	**Hvor er...?** voar ehr...
– the battleground	– **kamppladsen** <u>kahmp</u>·plas·sern
– the botanical gardens	– **den botaniske have** dehn boa·<u>ta</u>·nees·ker <u>ha</u>·ver
– the castle	– **slottet** <u>sloh</u>·derdh
– the downtown area	– **den indre by** dehn <u>in</u>·drah bew
– the fountain	– **springvandet** <u>spring</u>·van·nerdh
– the library	– **biblioteket** beeb·lee·oa·<u>teh</u>·kerdh
– the market	– **torvet** <u>toh</u>·werdh
– the museum	– **museet** moo·<u>say</u>·erdh
– the old town	– **den gamle bydel** dehn gahm·ler <u>bew</u>·dehl
– the palace	– **slottet** <u>sloh</u>·derdh
– the park	– **parken** <u>pah</u>·gern
– the ruins	– **ruinerne** roo·<u>ee</u>·nah·ner
– the shopping area	– **indkøbscentret** <u>in</u>·kurbs·sehn·tahdh
– the town square	– **rådhuspladsen** <u>rawdh</u>·hoos·pla·sern
Can you show me on the map?	**Kan du vise mig det på kortet?** kan doo <u>vee</u>·ser mie deh paw <u>kaw</u>·derdh

▶ For directions, see page 34.

Impressions

It's...	**Det er...** deh ehr...
– amazing	– **forbløffende** foh·<u>blur</u>·fern·der
– beautiful	– **smukt** smoakt
– boring	– **kedeligt** <u>keh</u>·dher·leet
– interesting	– **interessant** in·trah·<u>sant</u>
– magnificent	– **storartet** <u>stoar</u>·ah·derdh

112

– romantic	– **romantisk** roa·<u>man</u>·tisk
– strange	– **underligt** <u>oa</u>·nah·leet
– stunning	– **fantastisk flot** fan·<u>tas</u>·tisk floht
– terrible	– **frygteligt** <u>frurg</u>·ter·leet
– ugly	– **grimt** grimt
I *like/don't like* it.	**Jeg kan *lide/ikke lide* det.** yie kan *lee/ ig·ger lee* deh

Religion

Where's…?	**Hvor er…?** voar ehr…
– the cathedral	– **domkirken** <u>dohm</u>·keer·gern
– the church	– **kirken** <u>keer</u>·gern
– the mosque	– **moskeen** moa·<u>skeh</u>·ern
– the shrine	– **helgengraven** <u>hehl</u>·yern·gr<u>ah</u>·vern
– the synagogue	– **synagogen** sew·na·<u>goa</u>·ern
– the temple	– **templet** <u>tehmp</u>·lerdh
What time is *mass/ the service*?	**Hvad tid starter *messen/ gudstjenesten*?** vadh teedh <u>stah</u>·dah <u>meh</u>·sern/<u>goodhs</u>·tyeh·ner·stern

Shopping

Essential

Where is the *market/ mall [shopping centre]*?	**Hvor ligger *markedet/butikscentret*?** voar <u>li</u>·gah <u>mah</u>·ker·dherd/boo·<u>teeks</u>·sehn·tahdh
I'm just looking.	**Jeg ser mig bare omkring.** yie sehr mie b**ah** ohm·<u>kring</u>
Can you help me?	**Kan du hjælpe mig?** kan doo <u>yehl</u>·per mie

I'm being helped.	**Jeg får hjælp.** yie faw yehlp
How much?	**Hvor meget koster det?** voar <u>mie</u>·erdh <u>kohs</u>·dah deh
That's all, thanks.	**Det var det hele, tak.** deh vah deh <u>heh</u>·ler tahk
Where do I pay?	**Hvor kan jeg betale?** voar kan yie beh·<u>ta</u>·ler
I'll pay *in cash/by credit card.*	**Jeg vil gerne betale** *kontant/med* **kreditkort.** yie vil <u>gehr</u>·ner beh·<u>ta</u>·ler *kohn·<u>tant</u>/mehdh kreh·<u>deet</u>·kawd*
Can I have a receipt?	**Kan jeg få en kvittering?** kan yie fow ehn kvee·<u>teh</u>·ring

i

Denmark is an excellent country for shopping. Even in the capital, most shopping can be done on foot. Many of the major international retail stores are located in **Strøget** and **Købmagergade**, Copenhagen's main pedestrian streets. You can also check out **Vesterbro**, the western part of **Istegade** and the area around **Enghaveplads**. There, you'll find lots of trendy boutiques and pleasant cafes.

For everything under one roof, visit the **Magasin du Nord**, Scandinavia's largest department store, or the shopping malls: **Field's, Fisketorvet, Frederiksberg Centret** or **Illum**. Regular store hours are Monday to Friday from 9 a.m. to 5:30 p.m. On Friday stores are open until as late as 8 p.m. and Saturday they are generally open 10:00 a.m. to 4:00 or 5:00 p.m. Most stores are closed Sunday.

Stores

Where is…?	**Hvor er…?** voar ehr…
– the antiques store	– **antikvitetshandleren** an·tee·kvee·<u>tehts</u>·han·lahn
– the bakery	– **bageriet** ba·yah·<u>ree</u>·erdh
– the bank	– **banken** <u>bahnk</u>·ern
– the bookstore	– **boghandleren** <u>bow</u>·han·lahn
– the clothing store	– **tøjbutikken** <u>toi</u>·boo·tee·gern
– the delicatessen	– **delikatesseforretningen** de·li·ka·<u>tehs</u>·ser·foh·reht·ning·ern
– the department store	– **stormagasinet** <u>stoar</u>·mah·ga·s<u>ee</u>·nerdh
– the gift shop	– **gavebutikken** <u>ga</u>·ver·boo·tee·gern
– the health food store	– **helsekostforretningen** <u>hehl</u>·ser·kohst·foh·reht·ning·ern
– the jeweler	– **guldsmeden** <u>gool</u>·smeh·dhern

115

Where is...?	**Hvor er...?** voar ehr...
– the liquor store [off-licence]	– **vinhandelen** <u>veen</u>·han·lahn
– the market	– **markedet** <u>mah</u>·ker·dherd
– the pastry shop	– **konditoriet** kohn·dee·toh·<u>ree</u>·erdh
– the pharmacy [chemist]	– **apoteket** ah·poh·<u>teh</u>·kerdh
– the produce [grocery] store	– **købmanden** <u>kur</u>·man·ern
– the shoe store	– **skoforretningen** <u>skoa</u>·foh·reht·ning·ern
– the shopping mall [centre]	– **butikscentret** boo·<u>teeks</u>·sen·trahdh
– the souvenir store	– **souvenirbutikken** soo·veh·<u>neer</u>·boo·tee·kern
– the supermarket	– **supermarkedet** <u>soo</u>·pah·mah·kerdh
– the tobacconist	– **tobakshandlen** toa·<u>bahks</u>·han·lern
– the toy store	– **legetøjsforretningen** <u>lie</u>·er·tois·foh·reht·ning·ern

Services

Can you recommend...?	**Kan du anbefale...?** kan doo <u>an</u>·beh·<u>fa</u>·ler...
– a barber	– **en herréfrisør** ehn <u>hehr</u>·er·free·sur
– a dry cleaner	– **et renseri** eht rehn·ser·<u>ree</u>
– a hairstylist	– **en frisør** ehn free·<u>sur</u>
– a laundromat [launderette]	– **et vaskeri** eht vas·ger·<u>ree</u>
– a nail salon	– **en neglesalon** ehn <u>nie</u>·ler·sa·long
– a spa	– **en spa** ehn spa
– a travel agency	– **et rejsebureau** eht <u>rie</u>·ser·bew·roa

Can you…this?	**Kan du…det her?** kan doo…deh hehr
– alter	– **ændre** <u>ehn</u>·drah
– clean	– **rense** <u>rehn</u>·ser
– mend	– **reparere** reh·pah·<u>reh</u>·ah
– press	– **presse** <u>preh</u>·ser
When will it be ready?	**Hvornår er det klart?** voar·<u>naw</u> ehr deh klahd

Spa

I'd like…	**Jeg vil gerne have…** yie vil <u>gehr</u>·ner ha…
– an *eyebrow/bikini* wax	– **en øjenbrynsvoksning/bikinivoksning** ehn <u>oi</u>·ern·brewns·vohgs·ning/ bee·<u>kee</u>·nee·vohgs·ning
– a facial	– **en ansigtsbehandling** ehn <u>an</u>·sigts·beh·han·ling
– a *manicure/pedicure*	– **en *manicure/pedicure*** ehn ma·nee·<u>kew</u>·ah/peh·dee·<u>kew</u>·ah
– a (sports) massage	– **en (sports-)massage** ehn (<u>spohts</u>·)ma·<u>sa</u>·sher
Do you offer…?	**Tilbyder I…?** <u>tiil</u>·bew·dhah ee…
– acupuncture	– **akupunktur** ah·koo·poank·<u>toor</u>
– aromatherapy	– **aromaterapi** a·<u>roa</u>·ma·teh·rah·pee
– oxygen treatment	– **oxygenbehandling** ohk·sew·<u>gehn</u>·beh·han·ling
Do you have a sauna?	**Har I en sauna?** hah ee ehn <u>sow</u>·na

Many luxury hotels in Denmark offer spa and other health and beauty treatments. Spa resorts and destination spas may be found along the coast throughout Denmark. In recent years the Danish government has instituted rigorous regulations in regard to wellness centers, ensuring a top-quality stay.

Hair Salon

I'd like…	**Jeg vil gerne…** yie vil <u>gehr</u>·ner…
– an appointment for *today/tomorrow*	– **have en tid til *i dag/i morgen*** ha ehn teedh til ee da/ee <u>mohn</u>
– my hair styled	– **have mit hår sat** ha meet haw saht
– a haircut	– **klippes** <u>kli</u>·pers
– a trim	– **studses** <u>stoo</u>·sers
Don't cut it too short.	**Klip det ikke for kort.** klip deh <u>ig</u>·ger foh k**oh**t
Shorter here.	**Kortere her.** <u>koh</u>·dah·rah hehr

Sales Help

When does…*open/close*?	**Hvornår *åbner/lukker*…?** voar·naw <u>owb</u>·nah/<u>loa</u>·gah…
Where is…?	**Hvor er…?** voar ehr…
– the cashier [cash desk]	– **kassen** <u>ka</u>·sern
– the escalator	– **rulletrappen** <u>roo</u>·ler·trah·bern
– the elevator [lift]	– **elevatoren** eh·ler·<u>va</u>·tohn
– the fitting room	– **prøverummene** <u>prur</u>·ver·roa·mer·ner
– the store directory	– **butiksoversigten** boo·<u>teeks</u>·ow·ah·sig·tern
Can you help me?	**Kan du hjælpe mig?** kan doo <u>yehl</u>·per mie
I'm just looking.	**Jeg ser mig bare omkring.** yie sehr mie b**ah** ohm·<u>kring</u>
I'm being helped.	**Jeg får hjælp.** yie faw yehlp
Do you have any…?	**Har du nogen…?** hah doo <u>noa</u>·ern…
Can you show me…?	**Kan du vise mig…?** kan doo <u>vee</u>·ser mie…
Can you *ship/wrap* it?	**Kan du *forsende det/pakke det ind*?** kan doo foh·<u>seh</u>·ner deh/<u>pah</u>·ger deh in

How much?	**Hvor meget koster det?** voar <u>mie</u>·erdh <u>kohs</u>·dah deh
That's all, thanks.	**Det var det hele, tak.** deh vah deh h<u>eh</u>·ler tahk

▶ For clothing items, see page 124.

▶ For food items, see page 81.

▶ For souvenirs, see page 121.

You May Hear...

Kan jeg hjælpe dig? kan yie <u>yehl</u>·per die	Can I help you?
Lige et øjeblik. <u>lee</u>·er eht <u>oi</u>·er·blik	One moment.
Hvad skulle det være? vadj skoo deh <u>vay</u>·er	What would you like?
Skulle der være andet? skoo dehr <u>vay</u>·er <u>a</u>·nerdh	Anything else?

Preferences

I'd like something...	**Jeg vil gerne have noget...** yie vil <u>gehr</u>·ner ha n<u>oa</u>·erdh...
– cheap/expensive	– **billigt/dyrt** <u>bee</u>·leet/dewrt
– larger/smaller	– **mindre/større** <u>min</u>·drah/<u>stur</u>·ah
– from this region	– **fra dette område** frah <u>deh</u>·ter <u>ohm</u>·row·dher
Is it real?	**Er det ægte?** ehr deh <u>ayg</u>·der
Can you show me *this/that*?	**Kan du vise mig den *her/der*?** kan doo <u>vee</u>·ser mie dehn *hehr/dehr*

Decisions

It's not quite what I want.	**Det er ikke helt det, jeg vil have.** deh ehr <u>ig</u>·ger hehlt deh yie vil ha

I don't like it.	**Det bryder jeg mig ikke om.** deh <u>brew</u>·dhah yie mie <u>ig</u>·ger ohm
That's too expensive.	**Det er for dyrt.** deh ehr foh dewrt
I'd like to think about it.	**Jeg vil gerne tænke lidt over det.** yie vil <u>gehr</u>·ner <u>tehn</u>·ger lit <u>oh</u>·wah deh
I'll take it.	**Jeg tager det.** yie tah deh

Bargaining

That's too much.	**Det er for meget.** deh ehr foh <u>mie</u>·erdh
I'll give you...	**Jeg kan give dig...** yie kan gee die...
I only have...kroner.	**Jeg har kun...kroner.** yie hah koon... <u>kroa</u>·nah
Is that your best price?	**Et det den bedste pris, du kan tilbyde mig?** ehr deh dehn <u>behs</u>·der prees doo kan til·<u>bew</u>·dher mie
Can you give me a discount?	**Kan jeg få et nedslag i prisen?** kan yie fow eht <u>nehdh</u>·sla ee <u>pree</u>·sern

▶ For numbers, see page 162.

Paying

How much?	**Hvor meget koster det?** voar <u>mie</u>·erdh <u>kohs</u>·dah deh
I'll pay...	**Jeg vil gerne betale...** yie vil gehr·ner beh·<u>ta</u>·ler...
– in cash	– **kontant** kohn·<u>tant</u>
– by credit card	– **med kreditkort** mehdh kreh·<u>deet</u>·kawd
– by traveler's check [cheque]	– **med rejsecheck** mehdh <u>rie</u>·ser·shehk
Can I have a receipt?	**Kan jeg få en kvittering?** kan yie fow ehn kvee·<u>teh</u>·ring

You May Hear...

Hvordan ønsker du at betale? voar·<u>dan</u> urn·skah doo ad beh·<u>ta</u>·ler	How are you paying?
Kun kontant, tak. koon kohn·<u>tant</u> tahk	Cash only, please.

Complaints

I'd like... **Jeg vil gerne...** yie vil <u>gehr</u>·ner...

– to exchange this – **bytte det her** <u>bew</u>·der deh hehr

– to return this – **levere det her tilbage** leh·<u>veh</u>·ah deh hehr til·<u>ba</u>·yer

– a refund – **have mine penge tilbage** ha <u>mee</u>·ner pehng·er til·<u>ba</u>·yer

– to see the manager – **tale med bestyreren** <u>ta</u>·ler mehdh beh·<u>stew</u>·ahn

Souvenirs

aquavit	**akvavit** a·kvah·<u>veet</u>
amber	**rav** rahw
antiques	**antikviteter** an·tee·kvee·<u>teh</u>·dah
candles	**stearinlys** steh·<u>reen</u>·lews
ceramics	**keramik** keh·rah·<u>meek</u>
embroidery	**broderi** broa·dah·<u>ree</u>
furniture	**møbler** <u>murb</u>·lah
glassware	**en glasting** ehn <u>glas</u>·ting
handmade crafts	**kunsthåndværk** <u>koanst</u>·hown·vehrk
knitwear	**strikvarer** <u>strik</u>·vah·ah
hand-printed textiles	**håndtrykte tekstilvarer** <u>hawn</u>·trurg·der tehk·<u>steel</u>·vah·ah

May I see *this/that*?	**Må jeg se *den/det*?** mow yie seh *dehn/deh*
It's the one in *the window/display case*.	**Det er den i *vinduesudstillingen/ montren.*** deh ehr dehn ee *vin·doos·oodh·stil·ling·ern/mohn·tren*
I'd like…	**Jeg vil gerne have…** yie vil <u>gehr</u>·ner ha…
– a battery	**– et batteri** eht ba·der·<u>ree</u>
– a bracelet	**– et armbånd** eht **ahm**·bawn
– a brooch	**– en broche** ehn <u>broh</u>·sher
– earrings	**– et par ørenringe** eht pah <u>ur</u>·ahn·ring·er
– a necklace	**– en halskæde** ehn hals·**kay**·dher
– a ring	**– en ring** ehn ring
– a watch	**– et ur** eht oor
I'd like…	**Jeg vil gerne have…** yie vil <u>gehr</u>·ner ha…
– copper	**– kobber** <u>koh</u>·wah
– crystal	**– krystal** krew·<u>stal</u>
– diamonds	**– diamanter** dee·a·<u>mand</u>
– *white/yellow* gold	**– hvidguld/rødguld** <u>veedh</u>·gool/<u>rurdh</u>·gool
– pearls	**– perler** <u>pehr</u>·lah
– pewter	**– tinlegering** tin·leh·<u>sheh</u>·ring
– platinum	**– platin** pla·<u>teen</u>
– sterling silver	**– sterlingsølv** <u>stehr</u>·ling·surl
Is this real?	**Er det ægte?** ehr deh <u>ehg</u>·ter
Can you engrave it?	**Kan du indgravere det?** kan doo <u>in</u>·grah·veh·er deh

i Denmark is known for its modern design and quality craftsmanship around the world. You can peruse the fine silver and jewelry pieces at the **Georg Jensen** shops in Copenhagen and Århus. **Bang & Olufsen**, known internationally for its excellent audiovisual equipment, has shops throughout the country. **Ecco** shoes are easy to find and **Lego** is available in all toy and department stores. **Holmegård Glas, Stelton, Royal Copenhagen** and other well-known Danish designs can be purchased from interior design shops as well as department stores. Though your suitcase might not be big enough, Danes are also famous for their sleek and practical modern furniture.

Antiques

How old is this?	**Hvor gammelt er det?** voar gah·merlt ehr deh
Do you have anything from the…era?	**Har du noget fra…perioden?** hah doo noa·erdh fra…pehr·ee·oa·dhern
Will I have problems with customs?	**Får jeg problemer i tolden?** fow yie proa·bleh·mah ee toh·lern
Does it come with a certificate of authenticity?	**Følger der et ægthedscertifikat med?** furl·yah dehr eht ehgt·hehdhs·sehr·tee·fee·kat mehdh

Clothing

I'd like…	**Jeg vil gerne have…** yie vil gehr·ner ha…
Can I try this on?	**Må jeg prøve det?** mow yie prur·ver deh
It doesn't fit.	**Den passer ikke.** dehn pa·sah ig·ger
It's too…	**Den er for…** dehn ehr foh…
– big	**– stor** stoar
– small	**– lille** lee·ler
– short	**– kort** kawd
– long	**– lang** lahng
Do you have this in size…?	**Har du den i størrelse…?** hah doo dehn ee stur·erl·ser…
Do you have this in a *bigger/smaller* size?	**Har du den i en *større/mindre* størrelse?** hah doo dehn ee ehn stur·ah/min·drah stur·erlser

▶For numbers, see page 162.

You May See...

HERRETØJ	men's clothing
DAMETØJ	women's clothing
BØRNETØJ	children's clothing

Color

I'd like something... | **Jeg vil gerne have noget...** yie vil <u>gehr</u>·ner ha <u>noa</u>·erdh...

- beige — **beige** baysh
- black — **sort** soart
- blue — **blåt** blawht
- brown — **brunt** broonht
- gray — **gråt** grawht
- green — **grønt** grurnht
- orange — **orange** oa·<u>rang</u>·sher
- pink — **lyserødt** <u>lew</u>·ser·rurdht
- purple — **violet** vee·oa·<u>leht</u>
- red — **rødt** rurdht
- white — **hvidt** veedht
- yellow — **gult** g**oo**lt

Clothes and Accessories

backpack	**rygsæk** <u>rewg</u>·sehk
belt	**bælte** <u>behl</u>·der
bikini	**bikini** bee·<u>kee</u>·nee
blouse	**bluse** <u>bloo</u>·ser
bra	**bh** beh·<u>how</u>

125

coat	**frakke** <u>frah</u>·ger
dress	**kjole** <u>kyoa</u>·ler
hat	**hat** hat
jacket	**jakke** <u>yah</u>·ger
jeans	**cowboybukser** <u>kow</u>·boy·boag·sah
pajamas	**pyjamas** pew·<u>ya</u>·mas
pants [trousers]	**bukser** <u>boag</u>·sah
panty hose [tights]	**strømpebukser** <u>strum</u>·ber·boag·sah
purse [handbag]	**håndtaske** <u>hawn</u>·tas·ger
raincoat	**regnfrakke** <u>rien</u>·frah·ger
scarf	**tørklæde** <u>tur</u>·klay·dher
shirt	**skjorte** <u>skyoar</u>·der
shorts	**shorts** <u>shoh</u>ts
skirt	**nederdel** <u>neh</u>·dah·dehl
socks	**sokker** <u>soh</u>·gah
stockings	**strømper** <u>strum</u>·bah
suit	**sæt tøj** ♂ /**dragt** ♀ seht toi ♂ /drahgt ♀
sunglasses	**solbriller** <u>soal</u>·bri·lah
sweater	**sweater** <u>sveh</u>·dah
swimming trunks	**badebukser** <u>ba</u>·dher·boag·sah
swimsuit	**badedragt** <u>ba</u>·dher·drahgt
T-shirt	**t-shirt** <u>tee</u>·shurd
tie	**slips** slips
underwear	**underbukser** <u>oa</u>·nah·boag·sah

Fabric

I'd like…	**Jeg vil gerne have…** yie vil <u>gehr</u>·ner ha…
– cotton	– **bomuld** <u>boh</u>·mool
– denim	– **denim** <u>deh</u>·nim
– lace	– **blonde** <u>blohn</u>·der
– leather	– **læder** <u>lay</u>·dhah
– linen	– **lærred** <u>lehr</u>·erdh
– silk	– **silke** <u>sil</u>·ker
– wool	– **uld** ool
Is it machine washable?	**Kan det maskinvaskes?** kan deh ma·<u>skeen</u>·vas·gers

Shoes

I'd like…	**Jeg vil gerne have…** yie vil <u>gehr</u>·ner ha…
– *high-heeled/flat* shoes	– **et par *højhælede/flade* sko** eht pah <u>*hoi*</u>·*hay*·*ler*·*dher/fla*·*dher* skoa
– boots	– **støvler** <u>sturw</u>·lah
– loafers	– **hyttesko** <u>hew</u>·der·skoa
– sandals	– **sandaler** san·<u>da</u>·lah
– shoes	– **sko** skoa
– slippers	– **hjemmesko** <u>yeh</u>·mer·skoa
– sneakers	– **gummisko** <u>goa</u>·mee·skoa
In size…	**I størrelse…** ee <u>stur</u>·erl·ser…

▶ For numbers, see page 162.

Sizes

small	**lille** <u>lee</u>·ler
medium	**medium** <u>meh</u>·dee·oam

large	**stor** stoar
extra large	**ekstra stor** <u>ehk</u>·strah stoar
petite	**petit** peh·<u>teet</u>
plus size	**ekstra store størrelser** <u>ehk</u>·strah <u>stoa</u>·ah <u>stur</u>·erl·sah

Newsstand and Tobacconist

Do you sell English-language *books/newspapers*?	**Sælger I engelsksprogede *bøger/aviser*?** <u>sehl</u>·yah ee <u>ehng</u>·erlsk·spr<u>ow</u>·er·dher *<u>bur</u>·yah/a·<u>vee</u>·sah*
I'd like…	**Jeg vil gerne have…** yie vil <u>gehr</u>·ner ha…
– cigars	**– nogle cigarer** <u>noa</u>·ler see·<u>gah</u>·ah
– a *pack/carton* of cigarettes	**– en *pakke/karton* cigaretter** ehn *<u>pah</u>·ker/kah·<u>tong</u>* see·ga·<u>reh</u>·dah
– a lighter	**– en lighter** ehn <u>lie</u>·dah
– a magazine	**– et blad** eht bladh
– matches	**– nogle tændstikker** <u>noa</u>·ler <u>tehn</u>·sti·gah
– a newspaper	**– en avis** ehn a·<u>vees</u>
– a *road/town* map of…	**– et *vejkort/bykort* over…** eht *<u>vie</u>·kawd/<u>bew</u>·kawd* <u>oh</u>·wah…
– stamps	**– nogle frimærker** <u>noa</u>·ler <u>free</u>·mehr·kah

Photography

I'd like…camera.	**Jeg vil gerne have…kamera.** yie vil <u>gehr</u>·ner ha…<u>ka</u>·meh·rah
– an automatic	**– et automatisk** eht ow·toa·<u>ma</u>·tisk
– a digital	**– et digitalt** eht dee·gee·<u>talt</u>
– a disposable	**– et engangs-** eht <u>ehn</u>·gahngs-

I'd like…	**Jeg vil gerne have…** yie vil <u>gehr</u>·ner ha…
– a battery	**– et batteri** eht ba·der·<u>ree</u>
– digital prints	**– nogle digitaltryk** <u>noa</u>·ler dee·gee·<u>tal</u>·trurk
– a memory card	**– et hukommelseskort** eht hoo·<u>koh</u>·merl·sers·<u>kaw</u>d
Can I print digital photos here?	**Kan jeg udprinte digitale billeder her?** kan yie <u>oodh</u>·prin·der dee·gee·<u>ta</u>·ler <u>bil</u>·ler·dhah hehr

Sports and Leisure

Essential

When's the game?	**Hvornår starter kampen?** voar·<u>naw</u> <u>stah</u>·dah <u>kahm</u>·bern
Where's…?	**Hvor er…?** voar ehr…
– the beach	**– stranden** <u>strah</u>·nern
– the park	**– parken** <u>pah</u>·gern
– the pool	**– svømmebassinet** <u>svur</u>·mer·ba·sehng·erdh
Is it safe to *swim/dive* here?	**Er det sikkert at *svømme/dykke* her?** ehr deh <u>sig</u>·gahd ad *svur·mer/dur·ker* hehr
Can I rent [hire] golf clubs?	**Kan jeg leje golfkøller?** kan yie <u>lie</u>·er <u>gohlf</u>·kur·lah
How much per hour?	**Hvad koster det per time?** vadh <u>kohs</u>·dah deh pehr <u>tee</u>·mer
How far is it to…?	**Hvor langt er der til…?** voar lahngt ehr dehr til…
Can you show me on the map?	**Kan du vise mig det på kortet?** kan doo <u>vee</u>·ser mie deh paw <u>kaw</u>·derdh

Spectator Sports

When's...?	**Hvornår starter...?** voar·<u>naw</u> <u>stah</u>·dah...
– the basketball game	– **basketballkampen** <u>bah</u>·skerd·bowl·kahm·bern
– the boxing match	– **boksekampen** <u>bohk</u>·ser·kahm·bern
– the cycling race	– **cykelløbet** <u>sew</u>·kerl·lur·berdh
– the golf tournament	– **golfturneringen** <u>gohlf</u>·toor·<u>neh</u>·ing·ern
– the soccer [football] game	– **fodboldkampen** <u>foadh</u>·bohld·kahm·bern
– the tennis match	– **tenniskampen** <u>teh</u>·nees·kahm·bern
– the volleyball game	– **volleyballkampen** <u>voh</u>·lee·bawl·kahm·bern
Where's...?	**Hvor er...?** voar ehr...
– the horsetrack	– **hestevæddeløbsbanen** <u>hehs</u>·der·<u>vay</u>·dher·lurbs·<u>ba</u>·nern
– the racetrack	– **væddeløbsbanen** <u>vay</u>·dher·lurbs·ba·nern
– the stadium	– **stadiumet** <u>sta</u>·dee·oa·merdh
Where can I place a bet?	**Hvor kan jeg vædde?** voar kan yie <u>vay</u>·dher

i

Danes are very active people and most of the population participates in regular sporting activities. Sports can mean two things for Danes: **idræt** (an old Scandinavian word for sports) and **sport** (the contemporary term). **Idræt** often refers to the ideas of team-building and well-being associated with playing sports, while **sport** is related to the ideas of performance and athletic achievement.

If you are looking for an active vacation, you can find lots of opportunities for engaging in activities like cycling, sailing, soccer, handball, badminton, horseback riding, fishing and swimming, which are all popular. If you prefer to sit back and watch, sports are regularly broadcast on TV and there are many live events.

Participating

Where's…?	**Hvor er…?** voar ehr…
– the golf course	– **golfbanen** <u>gohlf</u>·ba·nern
– the gym	– **motionscentret** moa·<u>shoans</u>·cehn·tahdh
– the park	– **parken** <u>pah</u>·gern
– the tennis courts	– **tennisbanerne** <u>ten</u>·nis·ba·nah·ner
How much per…?	**Hvad koster det per…?** vadh kohs·dah deh pehr…
– day	– **dag** da
– hour	– **time** <u>tee</u>·mer
– game	– **spil** spil
– round	– **runde** <u>roan</u>·der
Can I rent [hire]…?	**Kan jeg leje…?** kan yie <u>lie</u>·er…
– golf clubs	– **golfkøller** <u>gohlf</u>·kur·lah
– equipment	– **udstyr** <u>oodh</u>·stewr
– a racket	– **en ketcher** ehn <u>keht</u>·shah

At the Beach/Pool

Where's the *beach/pool*?	**Hvor ligger *stranden/poolen*?** voar li·gah strah·nern/poo·lern
Is there…?	**Er der…?** ehr dehr…
– a kiddie [paddling] pool	– **et børnebassin** eht bur·ner·ba·sehng
– an *indoor/outdoor* pool	– **en *indendørs/udendørs* pool** ehn in·ern·durs/oo·dhern·durs pool
– a lifeguard	– **en livredder** ehn leew·ray·dhah
Is it safe…?	**Er det sikkert…?** ehr deh si·gaht…
– to swim	– **at gå i vandet her** ad gow ee van·erdh hehr
– to dive	– **at dykke her** ad dur·ker hehr
– for children	– **for børnene** foh bur·ner·ner

▶For travel with children, see page 141.

I want to rent [hire]…	**Jeg vil gerne leje…** yie vil gehr·ner lie·er…
– a deck chair	– **en liggestol** ehn lig·ger·stoal
– diving equipment	– **noget dykkerudstyr** eht dur·gah·oodh·stewr
– a jet-ski	– **nogle jetski** noa·ler jeht·skee
– a motorboat	– **en motorbåd** ehn moa·tah·bowdh
– a rowboat	– **en robåd** ehn roa·bawdh
– snorkling equipment	– **noget snorkleudstyr** noa·erdh snoh·kler·oodh·stewr
– a surfboard	– **et surfbræt** eht surf breht
– a towel	– **et håndklæde** eht hawn·klay·dher
– an umbrella	– **en parasol** ehn pah·rah·sohl
– water-skis	– **et par vandski** eht pah van·skee
– a windsurfer	– **en windsurfer** ehn win·sur·fer
For…hours.	**I…timer.** ee…tee·mah

Danes are fans of beach vacations and water sports. There are more than 270 marinas around the country and all different types of boats and other equipment can be rented. If you rent a jet-ski or windsurfer, keep in mind that, in an effort to protect the wildlife, Denmark has very strict rules regarding where they may be used.

Winter Sports

Where's the ice rink?	**Hvor er skøjtebanen.** voar ehr <u>skoi</u>·der·**ba**·nern
I'd like to rent ice skates.	**Jeg vil gerne leje et par skøjter.** yie vil <u>gehr</u>·ner <u>lie</u>·er eht pah <u>skoi</u>·dah
These are too *big/ small*.	**De er for *store/små.*** dee ehr foh <u>*stoa·ah*/ *smow*</u>
Are there lessons?	**Tilbyder I undervisning?** <u>til</u>·b**ew**·dhah ee <u>oa</u>·nah·**vees**·ning
How much?	**Hvor meget koster det?** voar <u>mie</u>·erdh <u>kohs</u>·dah deh

 The mild climate and topography of Denmark are not particularly good for winter sports. However, ice hockey and ice skating are popular.

In the Countryside

I'd like a map of…	**Jeg vil gerne have et kort over…** yie vil <u>gehr</u>·ner ha eht k**aw**d <u>ow</u>·ah…
– this region	– **dette område** <u>deh</u>·deh <u>ohm</u>·**row**·dher
– walking routes	– **vandreruter** <u>vahn</u>·drah·roo·dah
– bike routes	– **cykelruter** <u>sew</u>·kerl·roo·dah
– the trails	– **gangstier** <u>gahng</u>·stee·ah

Is it *easy/difficult*?	**Er det *nemt/svært*?** ehr deh *nehmt/svehrt*
Is it *far/steep*?	**Er det *langt herfra/stejlt*?** ehr deh *lahngt hehr·frah/stielt*
How far is it to…?	**Hvor langt er der til…?** voar lahngt ehr dehr til…
Can you show me on the map?	**Kan du vise mig det på kortet?** kan doo vee·ser mie deh paw <u>kaw</u>·derdh
I'm lost.	**Jeg er faret vild.** yie ehr <u>fah</u>·erdh veel
Where's…?	**Hvor er…?** voar ehr…
– the bridge	– **broen** <u>broa</u>·ern
– the cave	– **hulen** <u>hoo</u>·lern
– the cliff	– **klippen** <u>kli</u>·bern
– the farm	– **bondegården** <u>boa</u>·ner·gaw·ern
– the field	– **marken** <u>mah</u>·gern
– the forest	– **skoven** <u>skow</u>·ern
– the hill	– **bakken** <u>bah</u>·gern
– the lake	– **søen** <u>sur</u>·ern
– the nature preserve	– **naturreservatet** na·<u>toor</u>·reh·sah·va·derdh
– the overlook	– **udkigsposten** <u>oodh</u>·keegs·pohs·dern
– the park	– **parken** <u>pah</u>·gern
– the path	– **stien** <u>stee</u>·ern
– the picnic area	– **picnicområdet** <u>pik</u>·nik·ohm·<u>row</u>·dherd
– the pond	– **dammen** <u>dahm</u>·mern
– the river	– **floden** <u>floa</u>·dhern
– the sea	– **havet** <u>ha</u>·verdh
– the stream	– **åen** <u>ow</u>·ern

Culture and Nightlife

Essential

What is there to do in the evenings?	**Hvad laver man her om aftenen?** vadh <u>la</u>·vah man hehr ohm <u>af</u>·tern
Do you have a program of events?	**Har du et program over arrangementerne?** hah doo eht proa·<u>grahm</u> <u>ow</u>·ah ah·rahng·sheh·mang·ah·ner
What's playing at the movies [cinema] tonight?	**Hvad går der i biografen i aften?** vadh gaw dehr ee bee·oa·<u>gra</u>·fern ee <u>af</u>·tern
Where's…?	**Hvor er…?** voar ehr…
– the downtown area	– **den indre by** dehn <u>in</u>·drah bew
– the bar	– **baren** <u>bah</u>·ern
– the dance club	– **diskoteket** dees·koa·<u>teh</u>·kerdh
Is there a cover charge?	**Koster det noget at komme ind?** <u>kohs</u>·dah deh <u>noa</u>·erdh ad <u>koh</u>·mer in

Culturally, there is a lot to enjoy in Denmark. Ballet has been a tradition since the 17th century. The Royal Theater produces plays in a range of genres by both Danish and foreign playwrights. Danish film is also internationally known and has been dominated in recent years by Lars Von Trier.

If you are interested in the visual arts, visit the **Louisiana museum**. Located on the North Zealand coast, it is accessible by car or train. The museum houses an important collection of modern and contemporary art and is located on spectacular seaside property.

Entertainment

Can you recommend...?	**Kan du anbefale...?** kan doo <u>an</u>·beh·**fa**·ler...
– a concert	– **en koncert** ehn kohn·<u>sehrt</u>
– a movie	– **en film** ehn film
– an opera	– **en opera** ehn <u>oa</u>·peh·rah
– a play	– **et teaterstykke** eht teh·**a**·dah·stur·ger
When does it *start/end*?	**Hvad tid *starter/slutter* det?** vadh teedh <u>stah</u>·dah/<u>sloo</u>·dah deh
What's the dress code?	**Er der nogen regler for påklædning?** ehr dehr <u>noa</u>·ern <u>ray</u>·lah foh <u>pow</u>·klaydh·ning
I like...	**Jeg kan godt lide...** yie kan gohd lee...
– classical music	– **klassisk musik** <u>kla</u>·seesk moo·<u>seek</u>
– folk music	– **folkemusik** <u>fohl</u>·ker·moo·seek
– jazz	– **jazz** dj<u>a</u>s
– pop music	– **popmusik** <u>pohp</u>·moo·seek
– rap	– **rapmusik** <u>rahp</u>·moo·seek

▶ For ticketing, see page 21.

There are countless festivals scheduled throughout the year in Denmark. Tourist information offices, travel agencies, hotels and guide books offer extensive information about local as well as national celebrations. A handful of the annual events include the Copenhagen Marathon, Green Mermaid Festival, Beer Festival, Copenhagen Jazz Festival and Roskilde Festival of rock music. Also, if you're near the coast in June, Midsummer Night, the longest night of the year, is a fun event, traditionally celebrated with bonfires and other festivities.

You May Hear...

Sluk venligst din mobiltelefon.
sloak <u>vehn</u>·leest deen moa·<u>beel</u>·teh·ler·**foan**

Turn off your cell
[mobile] phones.

Nightlife

What is there to do in the evenings?	**Hvad laver man her om aftenen?** vadh <u>la</u>·vah man hehr ohm <u>af</u>·tern
Can you recommend...?	**Kan du anbefale...?** kan doo <u>an</u>·beh·**fa**·ler...
– a bar	– **en bar** ehn b**ah**
– a casino	– **et kasino** eht ka·<u>see</u>·noa
– a dance club	– **et diskotek** eht dee·skoa·<u>tehk</u>
– a gay club	– **et bøssediskotek** eht <u>bur</u>·ser·dee·skoa·**teh**k
– a nightclub	– **en natklub** ehn <u>nat</u>·kloob
Is there live music?	**Er der live musik?** ehr dehr <u>liev</u> moo·<u>seek</u>
How do I get there?	**Hvordan kommer jeg derhen?** voar·<u>dan</u> koh·mah yie dehr·<u>hehn</u>
Is there a cover charge?	**Koster det noget at komme ind?** <u>kohs</u>·dah det <u>noa</u>·erdh ad <u>koh</u>·mer in
Let's go dancing.	**Lad og gå ud og danse.** ladh ohs gow oodh ow <u>dan</u>·ser

A favorite Danish pastime is visiting pubs, though you can also find wine bars and cocktail bars. A traditional pub is called a **bodega** (beer bar). There you'll see Danes enjoying the local brews and playing dice. Dice can be requested at the bar.

Another option is to check out the many **hyggelige** cafes. Cafes range from those where you can order a drink and a simple sandwich to those with sophisticated decor and jet-set clientele.

If you're in the mood for music, there are plenty of dance clubs as well as regular live music shows to be found.

▼ Special Needs

Essential

I'm here on business.	**Jeg er her på forretningsrejse.** yie ehr hehr paw foh·<u>reht</u>·nings·rie·ser
Here's my business card.	**Her er mit visitkort.** hehr ehr meet vee·<u>seet</u>·**kaw**d
Can I have your card?	**Må jeg få dit visitkort?** mow yie fow deet vee·<u>seet</u>·**kaw**d
I have a meeting with…	**Jeg har et møde med…** yie hah eht <u>mur</u>·dher mehdh…
Where's…?	**Hvor er…?** voar ehr…
– the business center	– **businesscentret** <u>bis</u>·nis·sehn·tahdh
– the convention hall	– **konferencesalen** kohn·fer·<u>rahng</u>·ser·**sa**·lern
– the meeting room	– **mødelokalet** <u>mur</u>·dher·loa·ka·lerdh

Business Communication

I'm here to attend…	**Jeg er her for at deltage i et…** yie ehr hehr foh ad <u>dehl</u>·**ta**·yer ee eht…
– a seminar	– **et seminar** eht seh·mee·<u>nah</u>
– a conference	– **en konference** ehn kohn·fer·<u>rahng</u>·ser
– a meeting	– **et møde** eht <u>mur</u>·dher
My name is…	**Mit navn er…** meet nown ehr…
May I introduce my colleague…	**Må jeg præsentere dig for min kollega…** mow yie pray·sehn·<u>teh</u>·ah die foh meen koa·<u>leh</u>·ga…
I have *a meeting/an appointment* with…	**Jeg har *et møde/en aftale* med…** yie hah eht <u>mur</u>·dher/ehn <u>ow</u>·**ta**·ler mehdh…
I'm sorry I'm late.	**Jeg beklager, at jeg kommer for sent.** yie beh·<u>kla</u>·yah ad yie <u>koh</u>·mah foh sehnt

I need an interpreter.	**Jeg har brug for en tolk.** yie hah br**oo** foh ehn tohlk
You can reach me at the…Hotel.	**Du kan træffe mig på Hotel…** doo kan <u>treh</u>·fer mie paw hoa·<u>tehl</u>…
I'm here until…	**Jeg er her indtil den…** yie ehr hehr <u>in</u>·til dehn…
I need to…	**Jeg har brug for at…** yie hah br**oo** foh ad…
– make a call	– **lave en opringning** <u>la</u>·ver ehn <u>ohb</u>·ring·ning
– make a photocopy	– **tage en fotokopi** ta·er ehn <u>foa</u>·toa·koa·pee
– send an e-mail	– **sende en e-mail** <u>sehn</u>·ner ehn e·mail
– send a fax	– **sende en fax** <u>sehn</u>·ner ehn fahks
– send a package (overnight)	– **sende en pakke (ekspres)** <u>sehn</u>·ner ehn <u>pah</u>·ger (ehks·<u>prehs</u>)
It was a pleasure to meet you.	**Det glæder mig at træffe dig.** deh gl<u>ay</u>·dhah mie ad <u>treh</u>·fer die

▶For internet and communications, see page 46.

> *i* Danes tend to get right to business and don't engage in
> much small talk. When asked to give a briefing, be detailed,
> since Danes are rather meticulous. You'll find Danes to be
> comparatively serious and direct in business dealings and
> in their manner of speaking in general. This is not meant to
> insult. Though they are relatively informal, avoid comments
> that might be taken as personal.

You May Hear...

Har du en aftale? hah doo ehn <u>ow</u>·ta·ler	Do you have an appointment?
Med hvem? mehdh vehm	With whom?
Han/Hun **sidder i møde.** *han/hoon* <u>si</u>·dhah ee <u>mur</u>·dher	*He/She* is in a meeting.
Lige et øjeblik. <u>lee</u>·er eht <u>oi</u>·er·blik	One moment, please.
Sid ned. sidh nehdh	Have a seat.
Tak fordi du kom. tahk foh·<u>dee</u> doo kohm	Thank you for coming.

Travel with Children

Essential

Is there a discount for kids?	**Er det billigere for børn?** ehr deh <u>bee</u>·lee·ah foh burn
Can you recommend a babysitter?	**Kan du anbefale en babysitter?** kan doo <u>an</u>·beh·<u>fa</u>·ler ehn <u>bay</u>·bee·si·dah?
Can we have a *child's seat/highchair*?	**Må vi få** *et barnesæde/en høj stol***?** mow vee fow *eht <u>bah</u>·ner·<u>say</u>·dher/ehn hoi stoal*
Where can I change the baby?	**Hvor kan jeg skifte babyen?** voar kan yie <u>skeef</u>·der <u>bay</u>·bee·ern

Fun with Kids

Can you recommend something for the kids?	**Kan du anbefale noget til børnene?** kan doo <u>an</u>·beh·**fa**·ler <u>noa</u>·erdh til <u>bur</u>·ner·ner
Where's...?	**Hvor er...?** voar ehr...
– the amusement park	– **forlystelsesparken** foh·<u>lur</u>·stehl·sers·**pah**·kern
– the arcade	– **spillehallen** <u>spih</u>·ler·hal·lern
– the kiddie [paddling] pool	– **børnebassinet** <u>bur</u>·ner·ba·sehng·erdh
– the park	– **parken** <u>pah</u>·gern
– the playground	– **legepladsen** <u>lie</u>·er·pla·sern
– the zoo	– **den zoologiske have** dehn soa·<u>loa</u>·gee·sker <u>ha</u>·ver
Are kids allowed?	**Er der adgang for børn?** ehr dehr <u>adh</u>·gahng foh burn
Is it safe for kids?	**Er det sikkert for børnene?** ehr deh <u>si</u>·gaht foh <u>bur</u>·ner·ner
Is it suitable for... year olds?	**Egner det sig til...årige?** <u>ie</u>·nah deh sie til...**aw**·ree·yer

▶ For numbers, see page 162.

You May Hear...

Hvor er *han/hun* sød! voar ehr *han/hoon* surdh How cute *he/she* is!

Hvad hedder *han/hun*? vadh heh·dhah *han/hoon* What's *his/her* name?

Hvor gammel er *han/hun*? voar gah·merl ehr *han/hoon* How old is *he/she*?

Basic Needs for Kids ───────────

Do you have...?	**Har du...?** har doo...
– a baby bottle	– **en sutteflaske** ehn soo·der·flas·ker
– baby wipes	– **nogen vådservietter** noa·ern voadh·sehr·vee·eh·dah
– a car seat	– **et barnesæde** eht bah·ner·say·dher
– a children's *menu/portion*	– **en børnemenu/børneportioner** ehn bur·ner·meh·new/bur·ner·poh·shoa·nah
– a *child's seat/highchair*	– **et barnesæde/en høj stol** eht bah·ner·say·dher/ehn hoi stoal
– a crib	– **en barneseng** ehn bah·ner·sehng
– diapers [nappies]	– **nogen bleer** noa·ern bleh·ah
– formula	– **noget mælkeerstatning** noa·erdh mehl·ker·ehr·stad·ning
– a pacifier [soother]	– **en sut** ehn soot
– a playpen	– **en kravlegård** ehn krow·ler·gaw
– a stroller [pushchair]	– **en klapvogn** ehn klahp·vown
Can I breastfeed the baby here?	**Må jeg amme babyen her?** mow yie ah·mer bay·bee·ern hehr

| Where can I change the baby? | **Hvor kan jeg skifte babyen?** voar kan yie <u>skeef</u>·der bay·bee·ern |

▶ For dining with kids, see page 59.

Babysitting

Can you recommend a reliable babysitter?	**Kan du anbefale en pålidelig babysitter?** kan doo <u>an</u>·beh·**fa**·ler ehn paw·**lee**·dher·lee <u>bay</u>·bee·si·dah
What's the charge?	**Hvad koster det?** vadh <u>kohs</u>·dah deh
We'll be back by...	**Vi er tilbage klokken...** vee ehr til·<u>ba</u>·yer <u>kloh</u>·gern...

▶ For time, see page 164.

| I can be reached at... | **Jeg kan træffes på...** yie kan <u>treh</u>·fers pow... |

Health and Emergency

Can you recommend a pediatrician?	**Kan du anbefale en børnelæge?** kan doo <u>an</u>·beh·**fa**·ler ehn <u>bur</u>·ner·**lay**·er
My child is allergic to...	**Mit barn er allergisk overfor...** meet b**ah**n ehr a·<u>lehr</u>·gisk <u>ow</u>·ah·foh...
My child is missing.	**Mit barn er blevet væk.** meet b**ah**n ehr <u>bl**eh**</u>·werdh vehk
Have you seen a *boy/girl*?	**Har du set en *dreng/pige*?** hah doo seht ehn *drehng/<u>pee</u>·er*

▶ For food items, see page 81.

▶ For health, see page 150.

▶ For police, see page 148.

For the Disabled

Essential

Is there…?	**Er der…?** ehr dehr…
– access for the disabled	– **adgang for handicappede** <u>adh</u>·gahng for <u>han</u>·dee·kahp·per·dher
– a wheelchair ramp	– **en rampe til kørestole** ehn <u>rahm</u>·ber til <u>kur</u>·ah·st**oa**·ler
– a handicapped-[disabled-] accessible toilet	– **et handicaptoilet** eht <u>han</u>·dee·kahp·t**oa**·ee·lehd
I need…	**Jeg har brug for…** yie hah br**oo** foh…
– assistance	– **hjælp** yehlp
– an elevator [lift]	– **en elevator** ehn eh·ler·<u>va</u>·toh
– a ground-floor room	– **et værelse i stueetagen** eht <u>vehrl</u>·ser ee st**oo**·er·eh·<u>ta</u>·shern

145

Getting Help

I'm disabled.	**Jeg er handicappet.** yie ehr<u>han</u>·dee·kah·perdh
I'm deaf.	**Jeg er døv.** yie ehr durv
I'm *visually/hearing* impaired.	**Jeg er *synshæmmet/hørehæmmet*.** yie ehr <u>sew</u>ns·heh·merdh/<u>hur</u>·ah·hehm·merdh
I'm unable to *walk far/use the stairs*.	**Jeg kan ikke gå *langt/op ad trapperne*.** yie kan <u>ig</u>·ger gow *lahngt/ohb a <u>trah</u>·bah·ner*
Can I bring my wheelchair?	**Må jeg tage min kørestol med?** mow yie ta meen <u>kur</u>·ah·st<u>oa</u>l mehdh
Are guide dogs permitted?	**Er der adgang for førerhunde?** ehr dehr <u>adh</u>·gahng foh <u>fur</u>·ah·hoo·ner
Can you help me?	**Kan du hjælpe mig?** kan doo <u>yehl</u>·per mie
Please *open/hold* the door.	***Åbn/Hold* venligst døren.** *owbn/hohl* <u>vehn</u>·leest <u>dur</u>·ern

146

Resources

Emergencies

Essential

Help!	**Hjælp!** yehlp
Go away!	**Gå væk!** gow vehk
Stop thief!	**Stop tyven!** stohp <u>tew</u>·vern
Get a doctor!	**Tilkald læge!** <u>til</u>·kal <u>lay</u>·er
Fire!	**Det brænder!** deh <u>brahn</u>·nah
I'm lost.	**Jeg er faret vild** yie ehr <u>fah</u>·erdh veel
Can you help me?	**Kan du hjælpe mig?** kan doo <u>yehl</u>·per mie

Police

Essential

Call the police!	**Ring til politiet!** ring til poa·lee·<u>tee</u>·erdh
Where's the police station?	**Hvor ligger politistationen?** voar <u>li</u>·gah poa·lee·<u>tee</u>·sta·sh<u>oa</u>·nern
There has been an *accident/attack*.	**Der er sket *en ulykke/et overfald*.** dehr ehr skeht *ehn <u>oo</u>·lur·ker/eht <u>ow</u>·ah·fal*
My child is missing.	**Mit barn er blevet væk.** meet bahn ehr <u>bleh</u>·erdh vehk
I need...	**Jeg har brug for...** yie hah br<u>oo</u> foh...
– an interpreter	– **en tolk** ehn tohlk
– to contact my lawyer	– **at tale med min advokat** ad <u>ta</u>·ler mehdh meen adh·voa·<u>kat</u>
– to make a phone call	– **at lave en opringning** ad <u>la</u>·ver ehn <u>ohb</u>·ring·ning
I'm innocent.	**Jeg er uskyldig.** yie ehr oo·<u>skewl</u>·dee

You May Hear...

Udfyld venligst denne formular. <u>oodh</u>·fewl <u>vehn</u>·leest <u>deh</u>·neh foh·moo·<u>lah</u>	Fill out this form.
Hvornår/Hvor skete det? voar·<u>naw</u>/voar s<u>keh</u>·der deh	*When/Where* did it happen?
Hvordan ser *han/hun* ud? voar·<u>dan</u> sehr *han/hoon* oodh	What does *he/she* look like?

Lost Property and Theft

I want to report…	**Jeg vil anmelde…** yie vil <u>an</u>·meh·ler…
– a mugging	– **et overfald** eht <u>ow</u>·ah·fal
– a rape	– **en voldtægt** ehn <u>vohl</u>·tehkt
– a theft	– **et tyveri** eht tew·ah·<u>ree</u>
I've been *robbed/ mugged.*	**Jeg er blevet *bestjålet/overfaldet.*** yie ehr <u>bleh</u>·erdh beh·<u>styow</u>·lerdh/<u>ow</u>·ah·fa·lerdh
I've lost…	**Jeg har tabt…** yie hah tahbt
…has been stolen.	**…er blevet stjålet.** …ehr <u>bleh</u>·erdh <u>styow</u>·lerdh
– My backpack	– **Min rygsæk** meen <u>rewg</u>·sehk
– My bicycle	– **Min cykel** meen <u>sew</u>·gel
– My camera	– **Mit kamera** meet <u>ka</u>·meh·rah
– My (rental) car	– **Min (lejede) bil** meen (<u>lie</u>·er·dher) beel
– My computer	– **Min pc** meen peh·<u>seh</u>
– My credit cards	– **Mit kreditkort** meet kreh·<u>deet</u>·kawd
– My jewelry	– **Mine smykker** <u>mee</u>·ner <u>smur</u>·kah
– My money	– **Mine penge** <u>mee</u>·ner <u>pehng</u>·er
– My passport	– **Mit pas** meet pas
– My purse [handbag]	– **Min håndtaske** meen <u>hawn</u>·tas·ger

...has been stolen.	...er blevet stjålet. ...ehr bleh·erdh styow·lerdh
– My traveler's checks [cheques]	– Mine rejsechecks mee·ner rie·ser·shehk
– My wallet	– Min tegnebog meen tie·ner·bow
I need a police report for my insurance.	Jeg skal bruge en politianmeldelse til min forsikring. yie skal broo·er ehn poa·lee·tee·an·meh·lerl·ser til meen foh·sik·ring

Health

Essential

I'm sick [ill].	Jeg er syg. yie ehr sew
I need an English-speaking doctor.	Jeg har brug for en læge, der taler engelsk. yie hah broo foh ehn lay·er dehr ta·lah ehng·erlsk
It hurts here.	Det gør ondt her. deh gur ohnt hehr
I have a stomachache.	Jeg har mavepine. yie hah ma·ver·pee·ner

Finding a Doctor

Can you recommend a *doctor/dentist*?	Kan du anbefale en *læge/tandlæge*? kan doo an·beh·fa·ler ehn *lay·er/tan·lay·er*
Can the doctor come to see me here?	Kunne lægen komme for at se mig her? koo·ner lay·ern koh·mer foh ad seh mie hehr
I need an English-speaking doctor.	Jeg har brug for en læge, der taler engelsk. yie hah broo foh ehn lay·er dehr ta·lah ehng·erlsk
What are the office hours?	Hvornår er der åbent? voar·naw ehr dehr ow·bernt

Can I make an appointment…?	**Kan jeg få en tid…?** kan yie fow ehn teedh…
– for today	– **i dag** ee da
– for tomorrow	– **i morgen** ee mohn
– as soon as possible	– **så snart som muligt** saw snaht sohm moo·leet
It's urgent.	**Det haster.** deh has·dah

Symptoms

I'm…	**Jeg…** yie…
– bleeding	– **bløder** blur·dhah
– constipated	– **er forstoppet** ehr foh·stoh·berdh
– dizzy	– **er svimmel** ehr svim·merl
– nauseous	– **har kvalme** hah kval·mer
– vomiting	– **har kastet op** hah kas·derdh ohb
It hurts here.	**Det gør ondt her.** deh gur ohnt hehr
I have…	**Jeg har…** yie hah…
– an allergic reaction	– **en allergisk reaktion** ehn a·lehr·geesk reh·ahk·shoan
– chest pain	– **brystsmerter** brurst·smehr·dah
– an earache	– **ondt i ørerne** ohnt ee ur·ah·ner
– a fever	– **feber** feh·bah
– pain	– **smerter** smehr·dah
– a rash	– **fået udslet** fow·erdh oodh·sleht
– some swelling	– **fået en hævelse** fow·erdh ehn hay·vel·ser
– a stomachache	– **mavepine** ma·ver·pee·ner
– sunstroke	– **solstik** soal·stik
I've been sick [ill] for…days.	**Jeg har været syg i…dage.** yie hah vay·erdh sew ee…da·er

▶ For numbers, see page 162.

Health Conditions

I'm...	**Jeg har...** yie hah...
– anemic	– **blodmangel** <u>bloadh</u>·mahng·erl
– diabetic	– **sukkersyge** <u>soa</u>·gah·s**ew**·er
– asthmatic	– **astma** <u>ast</u>·ma

I'm allergic to *antibiotics/penicillin.*

Jeg er allergisk over for *antibiotika/ penicilin.* yie ehr a·<u>lehr</u>·geesk <u>ow</u>·ah·foh an·tee·bee·**oa**·tee·ka /pehn·see·<u>lee</u>n

▶ For food items, see page 81.

I have *arthritis/(high/ low) blood pressure.*

Jeg har *gigt/(højt/lavt) blodtryk.* yie hah geegt /(hoit /lavt) <u>bloadh</u>·trurk

I have a heart condition.

Jeg har en hjertesygdom. yie hah ehn <u>yehr</u>·der·s**ew**·dohm

I'm on...

Jeg tager... yie t**ah**...

You May Hear...

Hvad er der galt? vadh ehr dehr galt	What's wrong?
Hvor gør det ondt? voar gur deh ohnt	Where does it hurt?
Gør det ondt her? gur deh ohnt hehr	Does it hurt here?
Tager du nogen anden medicin? t**ah** doo <u>noa</u>·ern <u>a</u>·nern meh·dee·<u>seen</u>	Are you taking any other on medication?
Er du allergisk over for noget? ehr doo a·<u>lehr</u>·geesk <u>ow</u>·ah·foh <u>noa</u>·erdh	Are you allergic to anything?
Luk munden op. loak <u>moa</u>·nern ohb	Open your mouth.
Tag en dyb indånding. ta ehn d**ew**b <u>in</u>·own·ning	Breathe deeply.
Du skal indlægges på hospitalet til undersøgelse. doo skal <u>in</u>·lay·gers paw hoa·spee·<u>ta</u>·lerdh til <u>oa</u>·nah·<u>sur</u>·yerl·ser	I want you to go to the hospital.

Hospital

Please notify my family.	**Vær venlig og underret min familie.** vehr <u>vehn</u>·lee ow <u>oa</u>·nah·reht meen fa·<u>meel</u>·yer
I'm in pain.	**Jeg har smerter.** yie hah <u>smehr</u>·dah
I need a *doctor/nurse*.	**Jeg har brug for en *læge/ sygeplejerske.*** yie hah br<u>oo</u> foh ehn <u>lay</u>·er/<u>sew</u>·er·plie·ah·sker
When are visiting hours?	**Hvornår er der besøgstid?** voar·<u>naw</u> ehr dehr beh·<u>surs</u>·teedh
I'm visiting…	**Jeg er her for at besøge…** yie ehr hehr foh ad beh·<u>sur</u>·yer…

Dentist

I've *broken a tooth/lost a filling*.	**Jeg har *brækket en tand/tabt en plombe.*** yie hah <u>bray</u>·gerdh ehn tan/tabt ehn <u>ploam</u>·ber
I have a toothache.	**Jeg har tandpine.** yie hah <u>tan</u>·pee·ner
Can you fix this denture?	**Kan du reparere min protese?** kan doo reh·pah·<u>reh</u>·ah meen proa·<u>teh</u>·ser

Gynecologist

I have *menstrual cramps/a vaginal infection*.	**Jeg har *menstruationssmerter/ underlivsbetændelse.*** yie hah mehn·stroo·a·<u>shoans</u>·smehr·dah/ <u>oa</u>·nah·leevs·beh·teh·nel·ser
I missed my period.	**Jeg har ikke fået min menstruation.** yie hah <u>ig</u>·ger <u>fow</u>·erdh meen mehn·stroo·a·<u>shoan</u>
I'm on the Pill.	**Jeg tager p-piller.** yie tah <u>peh</u>·pil·lah
I'm (not) pregnant.	**Jeg er (ikke) gravid.** yie ehr (<u>ig</u>·ger) grah·<u>veedh</u>
I haven't had my period for…months.	**Jeg har ikke haft menstruation i… måneder.** yie hah <u>ig</u>·ger hahft mehn·stroo·a·<u>shoan</u> ee…<u>mow</u>·ner·dhah

▶For numbers, see page 162.

Optician

I've lost…	**Jeg har tabt….** yie hah tahbt…
– a contact lens	**– en af mine kontaktlinser** ehn a <u>mee</u>·ner kohn·<u>tahkt</u>·lin·sah
– my glasses	**– mine briller** <u>mee</u>·ner <u>bril</u>·lah
– a lens	**– en kontaktlinse** ehn kohn·<u>tahkt</u>·lin·ser

Payment and Insurance

How much?	**Hvor meget koster det?** voar <u>mie</u>·erdh <u>kohs</u>·dah deh
Can I pay by credit card?	**Kan jeg betale med kreditkort?** kan yie beh·<u>ta</u>·ler mehdh kreh·<u>deet</u>·kawd
I have insurance.	**Jeg er forsikret.** yie ehr foh·<u>sik</u>·erdh
Can I have a receipt for my insurance?	**Må jeg få en kvittering til min sygeforsikring?** mow yie fow ehn kvee·<u>teh</u>·ring til meen <u>sew</u>·er·foh·sik·ring

Pharmacy [Chemist]

Essential

Where's the nearest pharmacy?	**Hvor er det nærmeste apotek?** voar ehr deh <u>nehr</u>·meh·ster ah·poa·<u>tehk</u>
What time does the pharmacy *open/ close*?	**Hvornår *åbner/lukker* apoteket?** voar·<u>naw</u> <u>ow</u>b·nah/<u>loa</u>·gah ah·poa·<u>teh</u>·kerdh
What would you recommend for…?	**Hvad ville du anbefale mod…?** vadh <u>vee</u>·ler doo <u>an</u>·beh·<u>fa</u>·ler moadh…
Can you fill [make up] this prescription for me?	**Kan du give mig, hvad der står på recepten?** kan doo gee mie vadh dehr st<u>aw</u> pow reh·<u>sehp</u>·dern
I'm allergic to…	**Jeg er allergisk over for…** yie ehr a·<u>lehr</u>·geesk <u>ow</u>·ah foh…

154

In Denmark, an **apotek** (pharmacy) fills medical prescriptions, while a **parfumeri** sells non-prescription items, such as toiletries and cosmetics. Regular hours are Monday to Thursday from 9 a.m. to 5:30 p.m. Pharmacies may close at 7 p.m. on Fridays and 1 p.m. on Saturdays. At other times, pharmacies work on a rotating schedule. Check the store window to find the closest open pharmacy.

Dosage Instructions

How much should I take?	**Hvor meget skal jeg tage?** voar <u>mie</u>·erdh skal yie ta
How often?	**Hvor ofte?** voar <u>ohf</u>·der
Is it suitable for children?	**Egner det sig til børn?** <u>ie</u>·nah deh sie til burn
I'm taking…	**Jeg tager…** yie tah…
Are there side effects?	**Er der nogen bivirkninger?** ehr dehr <u>noa</u>·ern <u>bee</u>·veerk·ning·ah

You May See...

EN GANG/TRE GANGE DAGLIGT	*once/three times* a day
PILLER	tablets
DRÅBER	drops
TESKEER	teaspoons
FØR/EFTER/I FORBINDELSE MED ET MÅLTID	*before/after/with* meals
PÅ TOM MAVE	on an empty stomach
SLUG DEM HELE	swallow whole
KAN VIRKE DØSENDE	may cause drowsiness
KUN TIL UDVORTES BRUG	for external use only

Health Problems

I'd like some medicine for...
Jeg vil gerne have noget mod... yie vil <u>gehr</u>·ner ha <u>noa</u>·erdh moadh...

– a cold
– **forkølelse** foh·<u>kur</u>·lerl·ser

– a cough
– **hoste** <u>hoa</u>·ster

– diarrhea
– **diarré** dee·a·<u>reh</u>

– motion [travel] sickness
– **køresyge** <u>kur</u>·ah·s<u>ew</u>·er

– a sore throat
– **øm hals** urm hals

– sunburn
– **solforbrænding** <u>soal</u>·foh·breh·ning

– an upset stomach
– **dårlig mave** <u>daw</u>·lee <u>ma</u>·ver

Basic Needs

I'd like...
Jeg vil gerne have... yie vil <u>gehr</u>·ner ha...

– acetaminophen [paracetamol]
– **en æske paracetamol** ehn <u>ehs</u>·ker pah·rah·seh·ta·<u>moal</u>

– antiseptic cream	– **en antiseptisk creme** ehn <u>an</u>·tee·sehp·tisk krehm
– aspirin	– **en æske hovedpinepiller** ehn <u>ehs</u>·ger <u>ho</u>·wed·**pee**·ner·pil·lah
– bandages [plasters]	– **noget plaster** <u>noa</u>·erdh <u>plas</u>·dah
– a comb	– **en kam** ehn kahm
– condoms	– **nogle kondomer** <u>noa</u>·ler kohn·<u>doa</u>·mah
– contact lens solution	– **noget kontaktlinsevæske** <u>noa</u>·erdh kohn·<u>tahkt</u>·lin·ser·vehs·ger
– deodorant	– **deodorant** deh·oa·doa·<u>rahnt</u>
– hairspray	– **noget hårlak** <u>noa</u>·erdh <u>haw</u>·lahk
– ibuprofen	– **en æske ibuprofen** ehn <u>ehs</u>·ger ee·boo·proa·<u>fehn</u>
– insect repellent	– **en insekt-spray** ehn in·<u>sehkt</u>·spray
– a nail file	– **en neglefil** ehn <u>nie</u>·ler·<u>feel</u>
– a (disposable) razor	– **en barberskraber** ehn bah·<u>behr</u>·skrah·bah
– razor blades	– **nogle barberblade** <u>noa</u>·ler bah·<u>behr</u>·bla·dher
– sanitary napkins [pads]	– **nogle hygiejnebind** <u>noa</u>·ler hew·gee·<u>ie</u>·ner·bin
– shampoo/ conditioner	– **noget *shampoo/hårbalsam*** <u>noa</u>·erdh *shahm*·poa /<u>haw</u>·bal·sahm
– soap	– **et stykke sæbe** eht <u>stur</u>·ger <u>say</u>·ber
– sunscreen	– **noget solcreme** <u>noa</u>·erdh <u>soal</u>·krehm
– tampons	– **nogle tamponer** <u>noa</u>·ler tahm·<u>pong</u>·ah
– tissues	– **nogle papirlommetørklæder** <u>noa</u>·ler pah·<u>peer</u>·loh·mer·tur·k<u>lay</u>·dhah
– toilet paper	– **noget toiletpapir** <u>noa</u>·erdh toa·ee·<u>leht</u>·pah·peer

I'd like…	**Jeg vil gerne have…** yie vil <u>gehr</u>·ner ha…
– a toothbrush	– **en tandbørste** ehn <u>tahn</u>·bur·ster
– toothpaste	– **noget tandpasta** <u>noa</u>·erdh <u>tahn</u>·pas·ta

▶ For baby products, see page 143.

Reference

Grammar

Regular Verbs

The present tense of regular verbs in Danish is formed by adding
-r to the infinitive. The past tense is formed by adding **-de** to
the infinitive or **-te** to the root. The future is formed by using the
present tense of **ville** (will) + the verb in the infinitive. This applies
to all persons (e.g., I, you, he, she, it, etc.). Following are the
present, past and future forms of the verbs **at snakke** (to speak)
and **at spise** (to eat). The different conjugation endings are in bold.

	present	past	future
at snakke (to speak)	snakk**er**	snakke**de**	vil snakke
at spise (to eat)	spis**er**	spis**te**	vil spise

Irregular Verbs

There are a number of irregular verbs in Danish; these must
be memorized. Like regular verbs, however, the irregular verb
form remains the same, irrespective of person. Following are the
present, past and future conjugations for a number of important,
useful irregular verbs.

for. = formal	inf. = informal
sing. = singular	pl. = plural

	present	past	future
at være (to be)	er	var	vil være
at have (to have)	har	havde	vil have
at kunne (to be able)	kan	kunne	vil kunne
at gå (to walk)	går	gik	vil gå
at tage (to take)	tager	tog	vil tage

Nouns and Articles

The indefinite article (a, an) is expressed with **en** for common nouns and with **et** for neuter nouns. Generally, common nouns are those that can be both feminine and masculine (e.g. people, animals, etc.); neuter nouns have no gender (e.g. house, roof, etc.). However, note that there are several exceptions to this rule. Indefinite plurals are formed by adding **-e, -r** or **-er** to the singular.

	singular		plural	
common	**en pige**	a girl	**piger**	girls
neuter	**et hus**	a house	**huse**	houses

Some nouns remain unchanged in the plural, for example:

et rum	a room
rum	rooms

Definite articles: Where in English we say "the car", the Danes say the equivalent of "car-the", i.e. they tag the definite article onto the end of the noun. In the singular, common nouns take an **-en** ending, neuter nouns an **-et** ending. In the plural, both take an **-(e)ne** or **-(er)ne** ending.

	singular		plural	
common	**kanin**	the rabbit	**kaninerne**	the rabbits
neuter	**toget**	the train	**togene**	the trains

Pronouns

I	**jeg**
you (sing. inf./for.)	**du/De**
he	**han**
she	**hun**
it (common/neuter)	**den/det**
we	**vi**
you (pl.)	**I**
they	**de**

Word Order

Danish is similar to English in terms of word order for simple sentences: It follows the subject-verb-object pattern.

Example: **Vi efterlader vores bagage her.** We leave our luggage here.

When the sentence doesn't begin with a subject, the word order changes; the verb and the subject are inverted.

Questions are formed by reversing the order of the subject and verb:

Du ser bilen.	You see the car.
Ser du bilen?	Do you see the car?

Negation

A statement can be negated by inserting the word **ikke** after the verb:

Jeg taler dansk.	I speak Danish.
Jeg taler ikke dansk.	I do not speak Danish.

Imperatives

The imperative is exactly the same form as the stem of the verb:

Rejs!   Travel!   **Gå!**   Walk!

Tro!   Believe!   **Spis!**   Eat!

Adjectives

Adjectives usually precede nouns. In certain circumstances, the adjective takes an ending. In the singular indefinite form, adjectives remain unchanged but, in the plural indefinite form, with both common and neuter nouns, the adjective takes an **-e** ending.

	singular		plural	
common	en stor bil	a big car	store biler	big cars
neuter	et stort hus	a big house	store huse	big houses

In the definite form, an adjective takes an **-e** ending with both common and neuter nouns, in both the singular and plural. However, in this definite usage, **den** must be placed in front of the adjective in the case of common nouns in the singular, **det** in the case of singular neuter nouns and **de** with any plural.

	singular		plural	
common	**den** store bil	the big car	**de** store biler	the big cars
neuter	**det** store hus	the big house	**de** store huse	the big houses

Adverbs and Adverbial Expressions

Adverbs are generally formed by adding **-t** to the corresponding adjective.

Hun går hurtigt.   She walks quickly.

Hun går en hurtig tur.   She has a quick walk.

Numbers

Essential

0	**nul** noal
1	**en** ehn
2	**to** toa
3	**tre** treh
4	**fire** <u>fee</u>·ah
5	**fem** fehm
6	**seks** sehks
7	**syv** sew
8	**otte** <u>oa</u>·der
9	**ni** nee
10	**ti** tee
11	**elleve** <u>ehl</u>·ver
12	**tolv** toal
13	**tretten** treh·dern
14	**fjorten** <u>fyoar</u>·dern
15	**femten** <u>fehm</u>·dern
16	**seksten** <u>sie</u>·stern
17	**sytten** <u>sur</u>·dern
18	**atten** <u>a</u>·dern
19	**nitten** <u>ni</u>·dern
20	**tyve** <u>tew</u>·ver
21	**enogtyve** <u>ehn</u>·oh·**tew**·ver
22	**tooggyve** <u>toa</u>·oh·**tew**·ver
30	**tredive** <u>trehdh</u>·ver

31	**enogtredive** <u>ehn</u>·oh·trehdh·ver
40	**fyrre** <u>fur</u>·er
50	**halvtreds** hal·<u>trehs</u>
60	**tres** trehs
70	**halvfjerds** hal·<u>fyehrs</u>
80	**firs** feers
90	**halvfems** hal·<u>fehms</u>
100	**hundrede** <u>hoon</u>·rah·dher
101	**hundrede og et** <u>hoon</u>·rah·dher ow eht
200	**to hundrede** toa <u>hoon</u>·rah·dher
500	**fem hundrede** fehm <u>hoon</u>·rah·dher
1000	**tusind** <u>too</u>·sin
10,000	**ti tusind** tee <u>too</u>·sin
1,000,000	**en million** ehn meel·<u>yoan</u>

Ordinal Numbers

first	**første** <u>furs</u>·der
second	**anden/andet** <u>an</u>·ern/<u>an</u>·erdh
third	**tredje** <u>trehdh</u>·yer
fourth	**fjerde** f<u>yay</u>·ah
fifth	**femte** <u>fehm</u>·der
once	**en gang** ehn gahng
twice	**to gange** toa <u>gahng</u>·er
three times	**tre gange** treh <u>gahng</u>·er

Time

What time is it?	**Hvad er klokken?** vadh ehr <u>kloh</u>·gern
It's noon [midday].	**Klokken er tolv.** <u>kloh</u>·gern ehr tohl
At midnight.	**Ved midnat.** vedh <u>meedh</u>·nat
From nine o'clock to 5 o'clock.	**Fra klokken ni til sytten.** frah <u>kloh</u>·gern nee til <u>surd</u>·den
Twenty after [past] four.	**Tyve minutter over fire.** <u>tew</u>·ver mee·<u>noo</u>·dah ow·ah <u>fee</u>·ah
A quarter to nine.	**Kvart i ni.** kvaht ee nee
5:30 *a.m./p.m.*	**Halv seks om *morgenen/aftenen.*** hal sehks ohm *<u>moh</u>·nern/<u>af</u>·tern*

Days

Essential

Monday	**mandag** man·da
Tuesday	**tirsdag** teers·da
Wednesday	**onsdag** oans·da
Thursday	**torsdag** tohs·da
Friday	**fredag** freh·da
Saturday	**lørdag** lur·da
Sunday	**søndag** surn·da

Dates

yesterday	**i går** ee gaw
today	**i dag** ee da
tomorrow	**i morgen** ee mohn
day	**dag** da
week	**uge** oo·er
month	**måned** mow·nerdh
year	**år** aw

Months

January	**januar** ya·noo·ah
February	**februar** feh·broo·ah
March	**marts** mahts
April	**april** a·preel
May	**maj** mie
June	**juni** yoo·nee

July	**juli** <u>yoo</u>·lee
August	**august** ow·<u>goast</u>
September	**september** sehp·<u>tehm</u>·bah
October	**oktober** ohk·<u>toa</u>·bah
November	**november** noa·<u>vehm</u>·bah
December	**december** deh·<u>sehm</u>·bah

Seasons

spring	**forår** <u>foh</u>·aw
summer	**sommer** <u>sohm</u>·mah
fall [autumn]	**efterår** <u>ehf</u>·dah·aw
winter	**vinter** <u>vin</u>·dah

Holidays

January 1, New Year's Day	**Nytårsdag**
June 5, Constitution Day (afternoon only)	**Grundlovsdag**
December 24, Christmas Eve	**Juleaften**
December 25, Christmas Day	**Første juledag**
December 26, Boxing Day	**Anden juledag**

Moveable Dates

Maundy Thursday	**Skærtorsdag**
Good Friday	**Langfredag**
Easter Sunday	**Første påskedag**
Easter Monday	**Anden påskedag**

General Prayer Day	**Store Bededag**
Ascension Day	**Kristi himmelfart**

Conversion Tables ——————————————

Mileage

1 km = 0.62 mi	20 km = 12.4 mi
5 km = 3.10 mi	50 km = 31.0 mi
10 km = 6.20 mi	100 km = 61.0 mi

Measurement

1 gram	**gram** grahm	= 0.035 oz.
1 kilogram (kg)	**kilo** <u>kee</u>·loa	= 2.2 lb
1 liter (l)	**liter** <u>lee</u>·dah	= 1.06 U.S./ 0.88 Brit. quarts
1 centimeter (cm)	**decimeter** <u>deh</u>·see·meh·dah	= 0.4 inch
1 meter (m)	**meter** <u>meh</u>·dah	= 3.28 feet
1 kilometer (km)	**kilometer** <u>kee</u>·loa·meh·dah	= 0.62 mile

Temperature

-40° C – -40° F	-1° C – 30° F	20° C – 68° F
-30° C – -22° F	0° C – 32° F	25° C – 77° F
-20° C – -4° F	5° C – 41° F	30° C – 86° F
-10° C – 14° F	10° C – 50° F	35° C – 95° F
-5° C – 23° F	15° C – 59° F	

Oven Temperature

100° C – 212° F	177° C – 350° F
121° C – 250° F	204° C – 400° F
149° C – 300° F	260° C – 500° F

Useful Websites

www.visitdenmark.com
www.dt.dk
Official Danish tourism website

www.wonderfulcopenhagen.com
Official Copenhagen tourism website

www.dcu.dk
Danish Camping Union

www.copenhagen.com
City of Copenhagen website

www.berlitzpublishing.com
Berlitz Publishing website

www.sas.dk
Scandinavian Airlines

www.tsa.gov
*U.S. Transportation Security
Administration (TSA)*

www.caa.co.uk
UK Civil Aviation Authority (CAA)

www.hihostels.com
Hostelling International website

English–Danish Dictionary

A

a **(with common nouns)** en; **(with neuter nouns)** et

able kunne

about cirka

above ovenpå

accept *v* tage imod; **(approval)** godkende

access *n* adgang

accessory tilbehør

accident ulykke

account konto

ache smerte

acupuncture akupunktur

adapter adapter

address *n* adresse

admission adgang

admitted give adgang for

after efter

afternoon eftermiddag

aftershave lotion barbersprit

again igen

against mod

age alder

air conditioning klimaanlæg

air mattress luftmadras

airmail luftpost

airplane fly

airport lufthavn

aisle seat sæde ved midtergangen

alarm clock vækkeur

alcohol alkohol

alcoholic *adj* alkoholisk

allergic allergisk

allergic reaction allergisk reaktion

alphabet alfabet

also også

alter *v* ændre

altitude sickness bjergsyge

amazing forbløffende

amber rav

ambulance ambulance

American amerikaner

amethyst ametyst

amount *n* **(money)** beløb

amusement park forlystelsespark

analgesic smertestillende middel

and og

anesthetic narkose

animal dyr

ankle ankel

answer svar

antibiotic antibiotikum

adj	adjective	BE	British English
v	verb	n	noun

antidepressant antidepressivt middel

antique antikvitet

antiques store antikvitetshandler

antiseptic cream antiseptisk creme

any nogen

anyone nogen

anything noget

anywhere hvor som helst

apartment lejlighed

aperitif aperitif

appendix blindtarm

appliance udstyr

appointment aftale

arcade spillehal

architect arkitekt

arm arm

aromatherapy aromaterapi

around (approximately) omkring; (around the corner) rundt om

arrival ankomst

arrive ankomme

art kunst

art gallery kunstgalleri

aspirin hovedpinepille

assistance hjælp

assorted blandet

asthma astma

astringent sammentrækkende middel

at ved

ATM pengeautomat

attack n overfald

attend deltage

attractive køn

audio guide lydguide

Australia Australien

average gennemsnitlig

away væk

awful skrækkelig

B

baby baby

baby bottle sutteflaske

baby food babymad

baby wipes vådservietter

babysitter babysitter

back ryg

backache rygsmerter

backpack rygsæk

bad dårlig

bag (purse) taske; (shopping) pose

baggage [BE] bagage

baggage check bagageopbevaring

baggage claim bagagebånd

bakery bageri

balance (finance) saldo

balcony altan

ballet ballet

bandage n plaster

bank (finance) bank

bank note seddel

bar bar

barber herrefrisør

basket kurv

basketball game basketballkamp

bath bad

bathing suit badedragt

bathrobe badekåbe

bathroom badeværelse

battery batteri

battleground kampplads

be være

beach ball badebold

beard skæg

beautiful smuk

beauty salon skønhedssalon

bed seng

before (time) før

begin begynde

behind bagved

beige beige

bell (electric) ringeklokke

below nedenunder

belt bælte

berth køje

better bedre

between mellem

bicycle cykel

big stor

bike route cykelsti

bikini bikini

bill (restaurant) regning; (bank note) seddel

binoculars kikkert

bird fugl

birth fødsel

birthday fødselsdag

black sort

bladder blære

blade barberblad

blanket tæppe

bleach blegning

bleed bløde

blind (window) rullegardin

blister blist

blocked stoppet

blood blod

blood pressure blodtryk

blouse bluse

blow dry føntørre

blue blå

boat båd

boat trip bådtur

body krop

bone knogle

book bog

booklet (of tickets) rabatkort

bookstore boghandel

boot støvle

boring kedelig

born født

botanical garden botanisk have

botany botanik

bother genere

bottle flaske

bottle opener oplukker

bottom forneden

bowel tarm
bowl skål
box æske
boxing match boksekamp
boy dreng
boyfriend kæreste
bra bh
bracelet armbånd
brake *n* bremse
break (out of order) være i uorden
breakdown (car) få motorstop
breakfast morgenmad
breast bryst
breathe trække vejret
bridge bro
bring tage med
bring down få ned
British (person) brite; *adj* britisk
broken i stykker
brooch broche
broom kost
brown brun
bruise blåt mærke
brush *n* børste
bucket spand
bug insekt
build bygge
building bygning
burn brandsår
bus bus
bus station busstation
bus stop busholdeplads

business card visitkort
business center (at hotel)
  businesscenter
business class business class
business district
  forretningskvarter
business trip forretningsrejse
busy optaget
but men
butane gas flaskegas
butcher slagter
button knap
buy købe

C

cabin (ship) kahyt
cafe café
calculator regnemaskine
calendar kalender
call *n* (phone) opringning;
  v ringe; (summon) ringe efter
calm rolig
camera kamera
camera case fototaske
camera shop fotoforretning
camp bed campingseng
camp *v* campere
camping camping
camping equipment campingudstyr
campsite campingplads
can opener dåseåbner
can *v* (be able to) kan;
  n (container) dåse

Canada Canada
Canadian canadier
cancel annullere
candle stearinlys
candy store slikbutik
cap kasket
car bil
car hire [BE] biludlejning
car mechanic bilmekaniker
car park [BE] parkeringsplads
car rental biludlejning
car seat barnesæde
carafe karaffel
card kort
card game kortspil
cardigan cardigan
carry bære
cart indkøbsvogn
carton (of cigarettes) karton
case (camera) taske
cash *v* Indløse; *n* kontant
cashier kasse
casino kasino
castle slot; borg
caution forsigtig
cave hule
CD cd
cell phone mobiltelefon
cemetery kirkegård
center of town centrum
centimeter centimeter
ceramics keramik

certain vis
certificate attest
chair stol
change *n* **(money)** byttepenge;
  v **(money)** veksle; *v* **(clothes,
  diaper)** skifte
charcoal trækul
charge *n* gebyr; *v* koste
cheap billig
check (restaurant) *n* regning;
  (banking) check; *v* **(someone,
  something)** kontrollere; **(luggage)**
  tjekke ind
check-in desk (airport) check-in
  skranke
checking account checkkonto
check out *v* tjekke ud
check-up (medical)
  undersøgelse
cheers skål
chef køkkenchef
chemical toilet kemisk toilet
chemist [BE] apotek
cheque [BE] check
chess skak
chess set skakspil
chest brystkasse
chest pain smerter i brystet
child barn
child's seat barnesæde
children's clothing børnetøj
children's portion børneportion
choice valg

church kirke
cigar cigar
cigarette cigaret
cinema [BE] biograf
classical klassisk
clean adj ren; v gøre rent
cleansing cream rensecreme
clear v slette
cliff klippe
clip clips
clock ur
close v lukke
closed lukket
cloth stof
clothing tøj
clothing store tøjbutik
cloud sky
coat n (clothing) frakke
coin mønt
cold (illness) forkølelse; adj kold
collar flip
colleague kollega
color farve
comb kam
come komme
comedy lystspil
commission (fee) kommission
common (frequent) almindelig
compartment (train) kupé
compass kompas
complaint klage
computer computer; pc

concert koncert
concert hall koncertsal
condom kondom
conference room mødelokale
confirm bekræfte
confirmation bekræftelse
congratulations til lykke
connect v koble sig på
connection (transportation, internet) forbindelse
constipation forstoppelse
consulate konsulat
contact lens kontaktlinse
contagious smitsom
contain indeholde
contraceptive præventivmiddel
contract kontrakt
control kontrol
convention hall konferencesal
cooking facilities køkkenfaciliteter
copper kobber
corkscrew proptrækker
corner hjørne
cost n omkostning; v koste
cot klapseng
cotton bomuld
cough n hoste
counter disk
country land
countryside på landet
court house retsbygning
cover charge beregning per kuvert

cramps krampe
crayon farveblyant
cream (toiletry) creme
credit kredit
credit card kreditkort
crib barneseng
crockery [BE] spisestel
cross-country skiing langrend
crossing (maritime) overfart
crossroads vejkryds
crown (Danish currency) krone
crystal krystal
cufflink manchetknap
cuisine køkken
cup kop
currency valuta
currency exchange office
  vekselkontor
current (ocean) strøm
curtain gardin
customs told
customs declaration form
  toldangivelsesformular
cut *n* (wound) snitsår; *v* (with
  scissors) klippe
cut glass slebet glas
cycling race cykelløb

D

dairy mejeri
damaged beskadiget
dance club diskotek

dance *n* dans; *v* danse
danger fare
dangerous farlig
Danish (person) dansker; *adj* dansk
dark mørk
date (appointment)
  stævnemøde; (day) dato
day dag
decision beslutning
deck (ship) dæk
deck chair liggestol
declare (customs) fortolde
deep dyb
degree (temperature) grad
delay forsinkelse
delicatessen delikatesseforretning
delicious dejlig
deliver levere
delivery levering
denim denim
Denmark Danmark
dentist tandlæge
denture protese
deodorant deodorant
depart afgå
department (shop) afdeling
department store stormagasin
departure afgang
departure gate afgangsgate
deposit *n* (bank) indskud;
  (down payment) depositum
dessert dessert

detergent opvaskemiddel
detour (traffic) omkørsel
diabetic diabetiker
diamond diamant
diaper ble
diarrhea diarré
dictionary ordbog
diesel diesel
diet kost
difficult svær
digital digital
dining car spisevogn
dining room spisesalen
dinner middag
direct *adj* direkte; *v* (someone) vise vej til
direction vejangivelse
directory (phone) telefonbog
dirty beskidt
disabled handicappet
disc (parking) parkeringsskive
disconnect *v* (computer) koble sig fra
discount rabat
disease sygdom
dish (food item) ret
dishes (plates) spisetallerkner
dishwasher opvaskemaskine
dishwashing detergent opvaskemiddel
disinfectant desinficeringsmiddel
display case udstillingsmontre

district (of town) kvarter
disturb forstyrre
divorced skilt
dizzy svimmel
doctor læge
doctor's office lægekonsultation
dog hund
doll dukke
dollar (U.S.) dollar
domestic (airport terminal) indenrigs
domestic flight indenrigsfly
double bed dobbeltseng
double room dobbeltværelse
down ned
downtown area indre by
dozen dusin
dress *n* kjole
drink *n* drikkevare; (cocktail) drink; *v* drikke
drinking water drikkevand
drip dryppe
drive køre
driver's license kørekort
drop (liquid) dråbe
drugstore apotek
dry tør
dry cleaner renseri
dummy [BE] (baby's) sut
during i løbet af
duty (customs) told
duty-free goods toldfri varer

duty-free shop toldfri butik
dye farvning

E

each hver
ear øre
ear drops øredråber
earache ondt i ørerne
early tidligt
earring ørenring
east øst
easy nem
eat spise
economy class økonomiklasse
elastic elastik
electric elektrisk
electrical outlet stikkontakt
electricity elektricitet
electronic elektronisk
elevator elevator
e-mail e-mail
e-mail address e-mail-adresse
embassy ambassade
embroidery broderi
emerald smaragd
emergency nødstilfælde
emergency exit nødudgang
empty tom
enamel emalje
end slutning
engaged (phone) optaget
England England

English (language) engelsk;
  (person) englænder
enjoyable dejlig
enlarge forstørre
enough nok
enter *v* indtaste
entrance indgang
entrance fee entré
entry (access) adgang
envelope konvolut
equipment udstyr
eraser viskelæder
escalator rulletrappe
estimate *n* overslag;
  (quotation) tilbud
e-ticket e-billet
e-ticket check-in e-billet check-in
eurocheque eurocheck
Europe Europa
European Union Europæiske
  Fællesskab
evening aften
every hver
everything alt
exchange rate vekselkurs
exchange *v* (money) veksle
excursion udflugt
excuse *v* undskylde
exhibition udstilling
exit *n* udgang; *v* (computer) forlade
expect vente
expense udgift

expensive dyr
express ekspres
expression udtryk
extension (phone) lokal
extra ekstra
eye øje
eye drops øjendråber
eye shadow øjenskygge
eyesight syn

F

fabric (cloth) stof
face ansigt
facial ansigtsbehandling
factory fabrik
fair messe
fall *v* falde
family familie
fan ventilator
far langt
fare (ticket) billet
farm bondegård
far-sighted langsynet
fast *adj* hurtig
fast-food place burgerbar
faucet vandhane
fax fax
fax number faxnummer
fee (commission) kommission
feed *v* made
feel (physical state) føle
ferry færge

fever feber
few et par stykker
field mark
file (for nails) fil
fill in (form) udfylde
filling (tooth) plombe
film [BE] film
filter filter
find *v* finde
fine (OK) fint
fine arts kunst
finger finger
fire brand
fire door branddør
fire escape brandtrappe
fire exit nødudgang
first første
first-aid kit nødhjælpskasse
first class første klasse
first course forret
fishing fiskeri
fit *v* passe
fitting room prøverum
fix *v* reparere
flashlight lommelygte
flat [BE] (apartment) lejlighed
flatware bestik
flea market loppemarked
flight fly
floor etage
florist blomsterhandler
flower blomst

flu influenza
fluid væske
fog tåge
follow følge
food mad
food poisoning madforgiftning
foot fod
football [BE] fodbold
for for
forbidden forbudt
forecast vejrudsigt
foreign udenlandsk
forest skov
forget glemme
fork gaffel
form (document) formular
fountain springvand
frame (glasses) stel
free ledigt
freezer fryser
fresh frisk
friend ven
from fra
frost frostvejr
frying pan stegepande
full fuld
full-time fuldtids
furniture møbel

G

gallery galleri
game spil

garage garage
garbage skrald
garden have
gas benzin
gasoline benzin
gauze gaze
gem ædelsten
general almindelig
general delivery poste restante
general practitioner [BE]
  praktiserende læge
genuine ægte
get (find) komme til
get off stige af
get up stå op
gift gave
gift shop gavebutik
girl pige
girlfriend kæreste
give give
gland kirtel
glass (drinking) glas
glasses (optical) briller
glove handske
glue lim
go away gå væk
go back køre tilbage
go out gå ud
gold guld
golf club golfkølle
golf course golfbane
golf tournament golfturnering

good god
good afternoon goddag
good evening godaften
good morning godmorgen
good night godnat
goodbye farvel
gram gram
grandchild barnebarn
gray grå
great (excellent) storartet
Great Britain Storbritannien
green grøn
greengrocer's [BE]
  grønthandler
greeting hilsen
ground-floor room [BE]
  værelse i stueetagen
groundsheet teltunderlag
group gruppe
guesthouse pensionat
guide dog førerhund
guide *n* guide
guidebook rejsefører
gym motionscenter
gynecologist gynækolog

H

hair hår
hair dryer hårtørrer
hairbrush hårbørste
haircut klipning
hairdresser frisør

hairspray hårlak
hall (room) sal
hammer hammer
hammock hængekøje
hand hånd
hand cream håndcreme
hand washable vaske i hånden
handbag [BE] håndtaske
handicrafts kunsthåndværk
handkerchief lommetørklæde
handmade håndlavet
hanger bøjle
happy glad
harbor havn
hard hård
hardware store isenkræmmer
hare hare
hat hat
have (must) skulle; (possess) have
hay fever høfeber
head hoved
headache hovedpine
headlight billygte
headphones hovedtelefon
health food store
  helsekostforretning
health insurance sygeforsikring
hearing-impaired hørehæmmet
heart hjerte
heart attack hjerteanfald
heat *v* opvarme
heating varme

heavy tung

hello hej

helmet hjelm

help hjælp; (oneself) tage selv

here her

hi hej

high *adj* høj

high tide flod

highchair høj stol

highway motorvej

hill bakke

hire [BE] *v* leje

history historie

hole hul

holiday helligdag; [BE] ferie

home hjem

horseback riding ridning

hospital hospital

hot (temperature) varm

hotel hotel

hotel directory hotelfortegnelse

hotel reservation
 værelsesbestilling

hour (time) time

house hus

how hvordan

how far hvor langt

how long hvor længe

how many hvor mange

how much hvor meget

hug *v* kramme

hungry sulten

hunting jagt

hurry travlt

hurt gøre ondt

husband mand

I

I jeg

ice is

icy (weather) iskoldt

identification (card) id-kort

if hvis

ill [BE] syg

illness sygdom

important vigtig

imported importeret

impressive imponerende

in i

include iberegne

indoor indendørs

inexpensive billig

infected betændt

infection betændelse

inflammation betændelse

information information

information desk
 informationsluge

injection indsprøjtning

injure komme til skade

injury kvæstelse

inn kro

innocent uskyldig

inquiry forespørgsel

insect bite insektbid
insect repellent insekt-spray
insect spray insekt-spray
inside indenfor
instant messenger instant
   messenger
insurance forsikring
insurance claim forsikringskrav
interest (finance) rente
interested interesseret
interesting interessant
international international; (airport
   terminal) udenrigs
international flight udenrigsfly
internet internet
internet cafe internetcafé
interpreter tolk
intersection vejkryds
introduce præsentere
introduction (social)
   præsentation
investment investering
invitation indbydelse
invite *v* indbyde
invoice faktura
iodine jod
Ireland Irland
Irish (person) irlænder, *adj* irsk
iron n (clothing) strygejern;
   v stryge
itemized bill udspecificeret regning

J

jacket jakke
jar (container) glas
jaw kæbe
jazz jazz
jeans cowboybukser
jet ski jetski
jeweler guldsmed
join *v* komme med
joint (anatomy) led
journey rejse
just (only) bare

K

keep beholde
kerosene petroleum
key nøgle
key card nøglekort
kiddie pool børnebassin
kidney nyre
kilogram kilogram
kilometer kilometer
kind *adj* rar; *n* slags
kiss *v* kysse
knee knæ
knife kniv
knitwear strikvarer
knock banke på
know vide

L

label etiket
lace blonde
lactose intolerant laktoseintolerant
lake sø
lamp lampe
landscape landskab
language sprog
lantern lygte
large stor
last sidst
late (time) sent; (delay) forsinket
laugh grine
launderette [BE] møntvaskeri
laundromat møntvaskeri
laundry vasketøj
laundry facilities vaskerum
laundry service vaskeri
lawyer advokat
laxative afføringsmiddel
leather læder
leave v afgå; (behind) efterlade
left til venstre
left-luggage office [BE]
  bagageopbevaring
leg ben
lens (camera) objektiv; (glasses)
  linse
less mindre
lesson undervisning

letter brev
library bibliotek
license (driving) kørekort
life boat redningsbåd
life guard (beach) livredder
life jacket redningvest
life preserver redningsbælte
lift [BE] elevator
light (color) lys; (weight) let
light bulb pære
lighter lighter
lightning lyn
like vil gerne; (please) kan lide
linen lærred
lip læbe
lipstick læbestift
liquor store vinhandel
listen høre på
liter liter
little (amount) en smule
live v bo
loafers hyttesko
local lokal
log off logge af
log on logge på
login log ind
long lange
long-sighted [BE] langsynet
look v se
lose miste
loss tab

lost faret vild

lost and found hittegodskontor

lost property office [BE]
hittegodskontor

lotion lotion

loud (voice) høj

love v elske

lovely dejlig

low lav

low tide ebbe

luck lykke

luggage bagage

luggage cart bagagevogn

luggage locker bagageboks

lunch frokost

lung lunge

M

magazine blad

magnificent storartet

maid stuepige

mail n post; v poste

mailbox postkasse

make-up n sminke

mall butikscenter

mallet kølle

man mand

manager direktør

manicure manicure

many mange

map kort

market n market

married gift

mass (religious service) messe

massage massage

match n (sport) kamp

material stof

matinée eftermiddagsforestilling

mattress madras

may v må

meadow eng

meal måltid

mean v betyde

measure tage mål af

measuring cup målekrus

measuring spoon måleske

mechanic mekaniker

medicine (drug) medicin

meet mødes

memorial mindesmærke

memory card hukommelseskort

mend reparere

menu menu; menukort

message besked

meter meter

middle midten

midnight midnat

mileage kilometerpenge

minute minut

mirror spejl

miscellaneous forskellig

Miss frøken

miss v (lacking) mangle

mistake fejltagelse

mobile phone [BE] mobiltelefon
moisturizing cream
  fugtighedscreme
moment øjeblik
money penge
money order postanvisning
month måned
monument monument
moon måne
mop *n* moppe
moped knallert
more mere
morning morgen
mosque moské
mosquito net myggenet
motel motel
motorboat motorbåd
motorcycle motorcykel
motorway [BE] motorvej
moustache overskæg
mouth mund
mouthwash mundvand
move *v* flytte
movie film
Mr. hr.
Mrs. fru
much meget
mug *n* krus
mugging overfald
muscle muskel
museum museum
music musik

musical musical
must (have to) måtte

N

nail (body) negl
nail clippers negleklipper
nail file neglefil
nail salon neglesalon
name navn
napkin serviet
nappy [BE] ble
narrow smal
nationality nationalitet
natural naturlig
nausea kvalme
near nær
nearby i nærheden
near-sighted nærsynet
neck hals
necklace halskæde
need *v* brug for
needle nål
nerve nerve
never aldrig
new ny
newspaper avis
newsstand aviskiosk
next næste
next to ved siden af
nice (beautiful) dejlig
night nat
no nej

noisy støjende
none ingen
non-smoking ikke-ryger
noon middag
normal normal
north nord
nose næse
not ikke
note (bank note) seddel
notebook notesbog
nothing ikke noget
notice (sign) skilt
notify underrette
novice begynderniveau
now nu
number nummer
nurse sygeplejerske

O

o'clock klokken
occupation stilling
occupied optaget
office kontor
off-licence [BE] vinhandel
oil spiseolie
old gammel
old town gamle bydel
on på
on time til tiden
once en gang
one-way ticket enkeltbillet
only kun

open *adj* åben; *v* åbne
opera opera
operation operation
operator telefonist
opposite overfor
optician optiker
or eller
orange (color) orange
orchestra orkester; (seats) parket
order *n* bestilling; *v* bestille
out of order virker ikke
out of stock udsolgt
outlet (electric) stikkontakt
outside udenfor
oval oval
overlook *n* udkigspost
oxygen treatment
 oxygenbehandling

P

pacifier (baby's) sut
packet pakke
pad (sanitary) hygiejnebind
pail spand
pain smerte
painkiller smertestillende middel
paint *n* maling; *v* male
painting maleri
pair par
pajamas pyjamas
palace slot
palpitations hjertebanken

pants bukser
panty hose strømpebukser
paper papir
paper towel papirhåndklæde
parcel [BE] pakke
parents forældre
park *n* park; *v* parkere
parking parkering
parking disc parkeringsskive
parking garage parkeringskælder
parking lot parkeringsplads
parking meter parkometer
part del
part-time deltid
party (social gathering) fest
passport pas
passport control paskontrol
passport photo pasfoto
paste (glue) klister
pastry shop konditori
patch lappe
path sti
patient patient
pattern mønster
pay betale
payment betaling
peak *n* **(mountain)** bjergtop
pearl perle
pedestrian fodgænger
pediatrician børnelæge
pedicure pedicure
peg (tent) pløk

pen pen; kuglepen
pencil blyant
pendant vedhæng
penicillin penicillin
per day per dag
per hour per time
per person per person
per week per uge
percentage procentsats
perfume parfume
perhaps måske
period (monthly) menstruation
permit *n* **(fishing)** fiskekort;
  (hunting) jagtkort
person person
personal personlig
petite petit
petrol [BE] benzin
pewter tinlegering
pharmacy apotek
phone card telefonkort
photo billede
photocopy *n* fotokopi
photograph *n* billede
photography fotografering
phrase vending
pick up *v* **(go get)** hente
picnic medbragt mad
picnic basket madkurv
piece stykke
pill pille
pillow pude

PIN pinkode
pin n (brooch) nål
pink lyserød
pipe pibe
place n sted
plane fly
planetarium planetarium
plaster [BE] (bandage) plaster
plastic plastic
plastic bag plasticpose
plastic wrap plastikfolie
plate tallerken
platform [BE] (station) perron
platinum platin
play n (theatre) stykke; v spille
playground legeplads
playpen kravlegård
please vær venlig
plug (electric) stik
plunger svuppert; vaskesuger
pneumonia lungebetændelse
pocket lomme
point of interest seværdighed
point v pege
poison gift
poisoning forgiftning
pole (ski) skistav; (tent) teltstang
police politi
police report politianmeldelse
police station politistation
pond dam
pool svømmebassin

porcelain porcelæn
port havn
portable transportabel
porter portier
portion portion
post [BE] n post; v poste
post office posthus
postage porto
postage stamp frimærke
postcard postkort
pot gryde
pottery pottemageri
pound (British currency, weight) pund
powder pudder
pregnant gravid
premium (gas) 98 oktan
prescribe skrive recept på
prescription recept
present n gave
press (iron) presse
pressure tryk
pretty køn
price pris
price-fixed menu dagens menu
print n (photo) aftryk; v (document) udskrive
private privat
profit n overskud
program (of events) program
pronounce v udtale
pronunciation n udtale
provide skaffe

pull *v* trække
pump pumpe
puncture punktering
purchase *n* køb; *v* købe
pure ren
purple violet
purse (handbag) håndtaske
push *v* skubbe
pushchair [BE] klapvogn
put sætte

Q

quality kvalitet
quantity mængde
question *n* spørgsmål
quick hurtig
quiet stille

R

race væddeløb
race track væddeløbsbane
racket (sport) ketsjer
radio radio
railway station [BE] jernbanestation
rain regnvejr
raincoat regnfrakke
rape *n* voldtægt
rash udslet
rate n (exchange) vekselkurs;
  (price) takst
razor barbermaskine
razor blade barberblad

ready færdig
real (genuine) ægte
rear bagerst
receipt kvittering
reception reception
receptionist receptionist
recommend anbefale
rectangular rektangulær
red rød
reduction rabat
refrigerator køleskab
refund *v* få pengene tilbage
regards hilsner
region område
registered mail anbefalet
registration indskrivning
regular (gas) 95 oktan
relationship forhold
reliable pålidelig
religion religion
rent *v* leje
rental udlejning
rental car udlejningsbil
repair *n* reparation; *v* reparere
repeat *v* gentage
report (theft) anmelde
request *n* anmodning; *v* anmode
required nødvendig
requirement forespørgsel
reservation reservation
reservations office
  pladsreserveringen

reserve bestille

reserved reserveret

rest *n* rest

restaurant restaurant

restroom toilet

retired pensioneret

return (come back) komme tilbage;
(give back) returnere

return ticket [BE] returbillet

rib ribben

ribbon bånd

right (correct) rigtigt; (direction)
til højre

ring (jewelry) ring; (bell) ringe på

river flod

road vej

road assistance hjælp på vejen

road map vejkort

road sign vejskilt

robbery tyveri

romantic romantisk

room (hotel) værelse; (space) plads

room number værelsesnummer

room service roomservice; service
på værelset

room temperature rumtemperatur

rope reb

round rund

round (golf) runde

round-trip ticket returbillet

route rute

rowboat robåd

rubber (material) gummi

rubbish [BE] skrald

ruby rubin

S

safe n (vault) boks; (not in danger)
sikker

safety pin sikkerhedsnål

sailboat sejlbåd

sale *n* salg; (bargains) udsalg

same samme

sand sand

sandal sandal

sanitary napkin hygiejnebind

sapphire safir

satin satin

saucepan kasserolle

saucer underkop

sauna sauna

save *v* gemme

savings account
opsparingskonto

scarf tørklæde

scenery landskab

scenic route køn rute

school skole

scissors saks

scooter scooter

Scotland Skotland

screwdriver skruetrækker

sculpture skulptur

sea hav

season sæson

seat plads

seat belt sele

second sekund

second class anden klasse

second-hand shop
marskandiser; genbrugsbutik

section afdeling

see se

sell sælge

send sende

senior citizen pensionist

sentence sætning

separated (relationship)
separeret

serious alvorlig

serve (meal) servere

service (restaurant) betjening

set menu fast menu

sew sy

shampoo shampoo

shape form

sharp (pain) skarp

shave n barbering

shaving brush barberbørste

shaving cream barbercreme

shelf hylde

ship n skib; v forsende

shirt skjorte

shoe sko

shoe store skoforretning

shop n butik

shopping indkøb

shopping area indkøbscenter

shopping centre [BE]
butikscenter

shopping mall butikscenter

short kort

shorts shorts

short-sighted [BE] kortsynet

shoulder skulder

shovel n skovl

show n show; v vise

shower (stall) bruser

shrine helgengrav

shut lukket

shutter (window) skodde

side side

sightseeing sightseeing

sightseeing tour rundtur

sign underskrive

sign (notice) skilt; v underskrive

signature underskrift

silk silke

silver sølv

silverware sølvtøj

since siden

sing synge

single n (ticket) enkeltbillet;
(unmarried) ugift

single room enkeltværelse

size størrelse; (clothes) mål;
(shoes) nummer

skate v skøjte

skating rink skøjtebane

skin hud
skirt nederdel
sky himmel
sleep *v* sove
sleeping bag sovepose
sleeping car sovevogn
sleeping pill sovepille
sleeve ærme
slice *n* skive
slide (photo) dias
slipper hjemmesko
slow langsom
small lille
smoke ryge
smoker ryger
snack mellemmåltid
snack bar snackbar
sneaker gummisko
snorkeling equipment
  snorkeludstyr
snow sne
soap sæbe
soccer fodbold
soccer match fodboldkamp
sock sok
socket (electric) stikkontakt
soft blød
sold out udsolgt
someone nogen
something noget
song sang
soon snart
sore (painful) øm

sore throat ondt i halsen
sorry beklager
sort (kind) slags
south syd
souvenir souvenir
souvenir shop souvenirbutik
spa spa
spatula spatel
speak *v* tale
special særlig
specialist specialist
speciality specialitet
spell *v* stave
spend bruge
spine rygrad
sponge svamp
spoon ske
sport sport
sporting goods
  store sportsforretning
sprained forstuvet
square (shape) firkantet
stadium stadium
staff personale
stain plet
stainless steel rustfrit stål
stairs trappe
stamp *n* (postage) frimærke;
  v (ticket) stemple
staple hæfteklamme
star stjerne
start begynde
starter [BE] (meal) forret

station (train) jernbanestation; **(subway)** S-togsstation
stationery store papirhandel
stay (trip) ophold; *v* **(remain)** blive; *v* **(reside)** bo
steal stjæle
sterling silver sterlingsølv
sting *n* stik; *v* stikke
stockings strømpe
stomach mave
stomachache mavepine
stop (bus) busholdeplads; *v* stop
store (shop) forretning
store directory butiksoversigt
stove ovn
straight ahead ligeud
strange underlig
street gade
street map gadekort
string snor
stroller klapvogn
strong stærk
student studerende
study *v* studere
stunning fantastisk flot
sturdy solid
subway metro
subway map togkort
suit (man's) habit; **(woman's)** dragt
suitcase kuffert
sun sol

sunburn solforbrænding
sunglasses solbriller
sunstroke solstik
sun-tan lotion solcreme
super (gas) 98 oktan
supermarket supermarked
supplement *n* tillæg
suppository stikpille
surgery [BE] lægekonsultation
surname efternavn
swallow sluge
sweater sweater
sweatshirt sweatshirt
sweet sød
swell hæve
swelling hævelse
swim *v* svømme
swimming svømning
swimming pool svømmebasin
swimming trunks badebukser
swollen hævet
symbol symbol
synagogue synagoge
synthetic syntetisk
system system

T

table bord
tablet (medical) pille
tailor skrædder
take tage
take away *v* **[BE]** tage med

taken (occupied) taget
tampon tampon
tap (water) vandhane
tax skat
taxi taxa
taxi rank [BE] taxaholdeplads
taxi stand taxaholdeplads
team hold
tear v rive i stykker
teaspoon teske
telephone booth telefonboks
telephone directory telefonbog
telephone n telefon; v ringe
telephone number telefonnummer
tell sige
temperature temperatur
temple tempel
temporary midlertidig
tennis court tennisbane
tennis match tenniskamp
tennis racket tennisketsjer
tent telt
tent peg teltpløk
tent pole teltstang
terminal terminal
terrace terrasse
terrible frygtelig
terrifying
 skrækindjagende
thank takke
thank you tak
theater teater

theft tyveri
then så
there der
thermometer termometer
thief tyv
thigh lår
thin tynd
think (believe) tro
thirsty tørstig
thread tråd
throat hals
through gennem
thumb tommelfinger
thunder torden
thunderstorm tordenvejr
ticket billet
ticket office billetluge
tide ebbe
tie slips
tie clip slipseklemme
time n tid; (recurrent occasion)
 gang
timetable [BE] køreplan
tin [BE] (container) dåse
tin opener [BE] dåseåbner
tire dæk
tired træt
tissue papirslommetørklæde
to til
tobacco tobak
tobacconist tobakshandler
today i dag
toe tå

toilet [BE] toilet
toilet paper toiletpapir
toiletry toiletartikel
tomb gravsted
tomorrow i morgen
tongue tunge
tonight i aften
too (also) også
too much for meget
tool værktøj
tooth tand
toothache tandpine
toothbrush tandbørste
toothpaste tandpasta
torn (clothes) gået i stykker
touch v røre
tour tur
tourist office turistkontor
tow truck kranbil
towards mod
towel håndklæde
tower tårn
town by
town hall rådhus
toy legetøj
toy store legetøjsforretning
track (train) spor
traffic light trafiklys
trail gangsti
trailer campingvogn
train tog
tram sporvogn

tranquillizer beroligende middel
transfer (money) overførsel
translate oversætte
travel rejse
travel agency rejsebureau
travel guide rejsefører
travel sickness køresyge
traveler's check rejsecheck
treatment behandling
tree træ
trim studsning
trip rejse
trolley bagagevogn
trousers [BE] bukser
T-shirt T-shirt
tube tube
turn (change direction) drej til
turtleneck højhalset
TV fjernsyn
tweezers pincet

U

ugly grim
umbrella paraply; (beach) parasol
unconscious bevidstløs
under under
underground station [BE]
  metrostation
underpants underbukser
undershirt undertrøje
understand forstå
undress tage tøjet af
United States USA

195

university universitet
unleaded (fuel) blyfri
until indtil
up op
upstairs ovenpå
urgent haster
use brug
usually normalt

V

vacancy ledigt værelse
vacant ledig
vacation ferie
vaccinate vaccinere
vacuum cleaner støvsuger
valley dal
value værdi
value-added tax [BE] moms
vegetarian vegetar
vein vene
very meget
veterinarian dyrlæge
video camera videokamera
view (panorama) udsigt
village landsby
visit n besøg; v besøge
visiting hours besøgstid
visually impaired synshæmmet
V-neck V-hals
volleyball game volleyballkamp
voltage spænding
vomit v kaste op

W

wait v vente
waiter tjener
waiting room venteværelse
waitress kvindelig tjener
wake vække
wake-up call morgenvækning
Wales Wales
walk n gåtur
wall mur
wallet tegnebog
want vil have
warm (temperature) varm;
  v (reheat) opvarme
wash vaske
washing machine
  vaskemaskine
watch n ur
water vand
waterfall vandfald
waterproof vandtæt
water-ski vandski
wave n bølge
way vej
weather vejr
weather forecast vejrudsigt
week uge
weekend weekend
well godt
west vest
what hvad

wheel hjul
wheelchair kørestol
when hvornår
where hvor
which hvilken
white hvid
who hvem
whole hele
why hvorfor
wide brede
widow (female) enke; (male) enkemand
wife kone
wind vind
window vindue; (shop) butiksvindue
window seat vinduessæde
windsurfer windsurfer
wine list vinliste
wireless trådløs
wish v ønske
with med
withdraw (banking) få udbetalt
without uden
woman kvinde
wonderful vidunderlig

wood skov
wool uld
word ord
work v virke
worse værre
wound sår
write skrive
wrong forkert

X

X-ray røntgenfotografere

Y

year år
yellow gul
yes ja
yesterday i går
yet endnu
young ung
youth hostel vandrehjem

Z

zipper lynlås
zoo zoologisk have

Danish–English Dictionary

A

adapter adapter
adgang *n* access; admission; entry
adresse *n* address
advokat lawyer
afdeling *n* department (shop); section; entry
afføringsmiddel laxative
afgang departure
afgangsgate departure gate
afgå depart; leave
aftale appointment
aften evening
aftryk *n* print (photo)
akupunktur acupuncture
alder age
aldrig never
alfabet alphabet
alkohol alcohol
allergisk allergic
allergisk reaktion allergic reaction
almindelig common (frequent); general
alt everything
altan balcony
alvorlig serious
ambassade embassy
ambulance ambulance
amerikaner American

ametyst amethyst
anbefale recommend
anbefalet registered mail
anden klasse second class
ankel ankle
ankomme arrive
ankomst arrival
anmelde report (theft)
anmodning *n* request
annullere cancel
ansigt face
ansigtsbehandling facial
antibiotikum antibiotic
antidepressivt middel antidepressant
antikvitet antique
antikvitetshandler antiques store
antiseptisk creme antiseptic cream
apotek pharmacy [chemist BE]
arkitekt architect
arm arm
armbånd bracelet
aromaterapi aromatherapy
astma asthma
attest certificate
Australien Australia
automatgear automatic (car)
avis newspaper
aviskiosk newsstand

B

baby baby
babymad baby food

babysitter babysitter
bad bath
badebukser swimming trunks
badedragt bathing suit
badekåbe bathrobe
badeværelse bathroom
bagage luggage [baggage BE]
bagageboks luggage locker
bagagebånd baggage claim
bagageopbevaring baggage check
bagagevogn luggage cart [trolley BE]
bageri bakery
bagerst rear
bagved behind
bakke hill
ballet ballet
bane train
bank bank (finance)
banke på knock
bar bar
barberblad razor blade
barberbørste shaving brush
barbercreme shaving cream
barbering *n* shave
barbermaskine razor
barbersprit aftershave lotion
bare just (only)
barn child
barnebarn grandchild
barneseng crib
barnesæde car seat; child's seat
basketballkamp basketball game

batteri battery
bedre better
begynde begin; start
behandling treatment
beholde keep
beige beige
beklager sorry
bekræfte confirm
bekræftelse confirmation
beløb *n* amount (money)
ben leg
benzin gas [petrol BE]
beregning per kuvert cover charge
beroligende middel tranquillizer
beskadiget damaged
besked message
beskidt dirty
beslutning decision
bestik flatware
bestille *v* reserve; order
bestilling *n* order
besøg *n* visit
besøgstid visiting hours
betale pay
betaling payment
betjening service (restaurant)
betyde *v* mean
betændelse infection; inflammation
betændt infected
bevidstløs unconscious
bh bra
bibliotek library

bikini bikini
bil car
billede photo
billet ticket
billetluge ticket office
billig cheap
bilmekaniker car mechanic
biludlejning car rental [hire BE]
biograf movie theater [cinema BE]
bjergtop *n* peak (mountain)
blad magazine
blandet assorted
ble diaper [nappy BE]
blegning bleach
blindtarm appendix
blist blister
blod blood
blodtryk blood pressure
blomst flower
blomsterhandler florist
blonde lace
bluse blouse
blyant pencil
blyfri unleaded (fuel)
blød soft
bløde bleed
blå blue
blåt mærke bruise
bo *v* live
bog book
boghandel bookstore
boksekamp boxing match

bomuld cotton
bondegård farm
bord table
borg castle
botanisk have botanical garden
brand fire
branddør fire door
brandsår burn
brandtrappe fire escape
brede wide
bremse *n* brake
brev letter
briller glasses (optical)
brite British
bro bridge
broche brooch
broderi embroidery
brug use
brug for *v* need
bruge spend
brun brown
bruser *n* shower (stall)
bryst breast
brystkasse chest
bukser pants [trousers BE]
burgerbar fast-food place
bus bus
busholdeplads bus stop
business class business class
businesscenter business center
 (at hotel)
busstation bus station

butik *n* shop
butikscenter shopping mall [centre BE]
butiksoversigt store directory
by town
bygge build
bygning building
byttepenge *n* change (money)
bælte belt
bære carry
bøjle hanger
bølge *n* wave
børnebassin kiddie [paddling BE] pool
børnelæge pediatrician
børnemenu children's menu
børneportion children's portion
børnetøj children's clothing
børste *n* brush
båd boat
bådtur boat trip
bånd ribbon

C

café cafe
campere *v* camp
camping camping
campingplads campsite
campingseng camp bed
campingvogn trailer
Canada Canada
canadier Canadian

cardigan cardigan
cd CD
centimeter centimeter
centrum downtown area [centre BE]
check check [cheque BE] (banking)
check-in skranke check-in desk (airport)
checkkonto checking account
chokoladeforretning candy store
cigar cigar
cigaret cigarette
cirka about
clips clip
cowboybukser jeans
creme cream (toiletry)
cykel bicycle
cykelløb cycling race
cykelsti bike route

D

dag day
dagens menu price-fixed menu
dal valley
dam pond
dame lady
Danmark Denmark
dans *n* dance
dansk Danish (language, nationality)
dansker Danish (person)
dejlig delicious
del part
delikatesseforretning delicatessen

deltage attend
deltid part-time
denim denim
deodorant deodorant
der there
desinficeringsmiddel
 disinfectant
dessert dessert
diabetiker diabetic
diamant diamond
diarré diarrhea
dias slide (photo)
diesel diesel
direkte direct
direktør manager
disk counter
diskotek dance club
dobbeltseng double bed
dobbeltværelse double room
dollar dollar (U.S.)
drej til turn (change direction)
dreng boy
drikkevare *n* drink
dryppe drip
dråbe drop (liquid)
dukke doll
dusin dozen
dyb deep
dyr *adj* expensive; *n* animal
dyrlæge veterinarian
dæk deck (ship)
dårlig bad

dåse can [tin BE]
dåseåbner can [tin BE] opener

E

e-billet e-ticket
e-billet check-in e-ticket check-in
efter after
efterlade *v* leave (behind)
eftermiddag afternoon
eftermiddagsforestilling matinée
efternavn surname
ekspres express
ekstra extra
elastik *n* elastic
elektricitet electricity
elektrisk electric
elektronisk electronic
elevator elevator [lift BE]
eller or
elske *v* love
e-mail e-mail
e-mail-adresse e-mail address
emalje enamel
en a (with common nouns)
en gang once
en masse lot (a lot)
en smule little (amount)
endnu yet
eng meadow
engelsk English (language)
England England
englænder English (person)

enke widow (male)
enkemand widow (female)
enkeltbillet one-way [single BE] ticket
enkeltværelse single room
entré entrance fee
et a (with neuter nouns)
et par stykker few
etage floor
etiket label
eurocheck eurocheque
Europa Europe
Europæiske Fællesskab European Union

F

fabrik factory
faktura invoice
familie family
fantastisk flot stunning
fare danger
faret vild lost
farlig dangerous
farve color
farveblyant crayon
farvel goodbye
farvning dye
fast menu set menu
fax fax
faxnummer fax number
feber fever
fejltagelse mistake

ferie vacation
fest party (social gathering)
fil file (for nails)
film movie [film BE]
filter filter
finde find
finger finger
firkantet square (shape)
fiskekort *n* permit (fishing)
fiskeri fishing
fjernsyn TV
flaske bottle
flaskegas butane gas
flip collar
flod river; high tide
flonel flannel
fly airplane; flight
flytte *v* move
fod foot
fodbold soccer [football BE]
fodboldkamp soccer [football BE] match
fodgænger pedestrian
for for
for meget too much
for varm overheated (engine)
forbindelse connection (transportation, internet)
forbløffende amazing
forbudt forbidden
forældre parents
færdig ready

færge ferry
fødsel birth
fødselsdag birthday
født born
føle feel (physical state)
følge follow
føntørre blow-dry
før before (time)
førerhund guide dog
få motorstop breakdown (car)
få ned bring down
få pengene tilbage *v* refund
få udbetalt withdraw (banking)

G

gade street
gadekort street map
gaffel fork
galleri gallery
gamle bydel old town
gammel old
gang *n* time (recurrent occasion)
gangsti trail
garage garage
gardin curtain
gave gift; present
gavebutik gift shop
gaze gauze
gebyr *n* charge
gemme *v* save
genbrugsbutik second-hand shop
genere bother

gennem through
gennemsnitlig average
gentage *v* repeat
gift *adj* married; *n* poison
give give
give adgang for admitted
glad happy
glas glass; jar (container)
glemme forget
god good
godaften good evening
goddag good afternoon
godmorgen good morning
godnat good night
godt fine (OK); well
golfbane golf course
golfkølle golf club
golfturnering golf tournament
grad degree (temperature)
gram gram
grammatik grammar
gravid pregnant
gravsted tomb
grim ugly
grine laugh
gruppe group
gryde pot
grøn green
grønthandler produce store
  [greengrocer's BE]
grå gray
guide *n* guide

gul yellow
guld gold
guldsmed jeweler
gummi rubber (material)
gummisko sneaker
gynækolog gynecologist
gøre ondt hurt
gøre rent *v* clean
gå ud go out
gå væk go away
gåtur *n* walk

H

hals neck; throat
halskæde necklace
hammer hammer
handicappet disabled
handske glove
hare hare
haste urgent
hat hat
hav sea
have garden
havn harbor; port
hej hello; hi
hele whole
helgengrav shrine
helligdag holiday (public)
helsekostforretning health food
  store
hente *v* pick up (go get)
her here

herrefrisør barber
hilsen greeting
hilsner regards
himmel sky
historie history
hittegodskontor lost and found
  [lost property office BE]
hjelm helmet
hjem home
hjemmesko slipper
hjerte heart
hjerteanfald heart attack
hjertebanken palpitations
hjul wheel
hjælp assistance; help
hjælp på vejen roadside assistance
hjørne corner
hold team
hospital hospital
hoste *n* cough
hotel hotel
hotelfortegnelse hotel directory
hoved head
hovedpine headache
hovedpinepille aspirin
hovedtelefon headphones
hr. Mr.
hud skin
hukommelseskort memory card
hul hole
hule cave
hund dog

hurtig *adj* fast; quick
hus house
husholdningsartikel household item
hvad what
hvem who
hver each; every
hvid white
hvilken which
hvis if
hvor where
hvor langt how far
hvor længe how long
hvor mange how many
hvor meget how much
hvor som helst anywhere
hvordan how
hvorfor why
hvornår when
hygiejnebind sanitary napkin
  [pad BE]
hylde shelf
hyttesko loafers
hæfteklamme staple
hængekøje hammock
hæve swell
hævelse swelling
hævet swollen
høfeber hay fever
høj high; loud (volume)
høj stol highchair
højhalset turtleneck
høre på listen

hørehæmmet hearing impaired
hånd hand
håndcreme hand cream
håndklæde towel
håndlavet handmade
håndtaske purse [handbag BE]
hår hair
hårbørste hairbrush
hård hard
hårlak hairspray
hårtørrer hair dryer

I

i aften tonight
i dag today
i går yesterday
i løbet af during
i morgen tomorrow
i nærheden nearby
i stykker broken
iberegne include
id-kort identification (card)
igen again
ikke not
ikke noget nothing
ikke-ryger non-smoking
imponerende impressive
importeret imported
indbyde *v* invite
indbydelse invitation
indeholde contain
indendørs indoor

indenfor inside
indenrigs domestic
(airport terminal)
indenrigsfly domestic flight
indgang entrance
indkøb shopping
indkøbscenter shopping area
indkøbsvogn cart
indløse v cash
indre by downtown area
indskrivning registration
indskud n deposit (bank)
indsprøjtning injection
indtaste v enter
indtil until
influenza flu
information information
informationsluge information desk
ingen none
insekt bug
insektbid insect bite
insekt-spray insect repellent
instant messenger instant
messenger
interessant interesting
interesseret interested
international international
(airport terminal)
internet internet
internetcafé internet cafe
investering investment
Irland Ireland

irlænder Irish
isenkræmmer hardware store
iskoldt icy (weather)

J

ja yes
jagt hunting
jakke jacket
jazz jazz
jeg I
jernbanestation train
[railway BE] station
jetski jet ski
jod iodine

K

kahyt cabin (ship)
kalender calendar
kam comb
kamera camera
kamp n match (sport)
kampplads battleground
kan v can (be able to)
kapel chapel
karaffel carafe
karton carton (of cigarettes)
kasino casino
kasket cap
kasse cash desk; cashier
kasserolle saucepan
kedelig boring
kemisk toilet chemical toilet

keramik ceramics
ketsjer racket (sport)
kikkert binoculars
kilde *n* spring (water)
kilogram kilogram
kilometer kilometer
kilometerpenge mileage
kirke church
kirkegård cemetery
kirtel gland
kjole *n* dress
klage complaint
klapseng cot
klapvogn stroller [pushchair BE]
klassisk classical
klimaanlæg air conditioning
klipning haircut
klister paste (glue)
klokken o'clock
knallert moped
knap button
kniv knife
knogle bone
knæ knee
kobber copper
koble sig fra *v* disconnect
  (computer)
koble sig på *v* connect (computer)
kollega colleague
komme come
komme med join
komme til get (find)

komme til skade injure
komme tilbage return (give back)
kommission commission (fee)
kompas compass
koncert concert
koncertsal concert hall
konditori pastry shop
kondom condom
kone wife
konferencesal convention hall
konsulat consulate
kontaktlinse contact lens
konto account
kontor office
kontrakt contract
kontrol control
konvolut envelope
kop cup
kort card; map; *adj* short
kortspil card game
kortsynet near-sighted
  [short-sighted BE]
kost diet
kost broom
kramme *v* hug
krampe cramps
kranbil tow truck
kravlegård playpen
kredit credit
kreditkort credit card
kro inn
krone crown (Danish currency)

krop body
krus *n* mug (cup)
krystal crystal
kuffert suitcase
kuglepen pen
kun only
kunne able
kunst art
kunstgalleri art gallery
kunsthåndværk handicrafts
kupé compartment (train)
kurv basket
kvalitet quality
kvalme nausea
kvarter district (of town)
kvinde woman
kvindelig tjener waitress
kvittering receipt
kvæstelse injury
kysse *v* kiss
kæbe jaw
kæreste boyfriend; girlfriend
køb *n* purchase
købe buy
køje berth
køkken cuisine
køkkenchef chef
køkkenfaciliteter cooking facilities
køleskab refrigerator
kølle mallet
køn attractive; pretty
køn rute scenic route

køre drive
køre tilbage go back
kørekort driver's license
køreplan schedule [timetable BE]
kørestol wheelchair
køresyge travel sickness

L

laktoseintolerant lactose intolerant
lampe lamp
land country
landsby village
landskab landscape; scenery
lange long
langrend cross-country skiing
langsom slow
langsynet far-sighted
  [long-sighted BE]
langt far
lappe patch
lav low
led *n* joint (anatomy)
ledig vacant
ledigt free
ledigt værelse vacancy
legeplads playground
legetøj toy
legetøjsforretning toy store
leje *v* rent [hire BE]
lejlighed apartment [flat BE]
let light (weight)
levere deliver

levering delivery
ligeud straight ahead
liggestol deck chair
lighter lighter
lille small
lim glue
liter liter
livredder life guard (beach)
log ind login
logge af log off
logge på log on
lokal extension (phone); local
lomme pocket
lommelygte flashlight
lommetørklæde handkerchief
loppemarked flea market
lotion lotion
lufthavn airport
luftmadras air mattress
luftpost airmail
lukke v close
lunge lung
lungebetændelse pneumonia
lydguide audio guide
lygte lantern
lykke luck
lyn lightning
lynlås zipper
lys light (color)
lyserød pink
lystspil comedy
læbe lip

læbestift lipstick
læder leather
læge doctor
lægekonsultation doctor's office [surgery BE]
lærred linen
lår thigh

M

mad food
made v feed
madforgiftning food poisoning
madkurv picnic basket
madras mattress
maleri painting
maling n paint
manchetknap cufflink
mand husband; man
mange many
mangle v miss (lacking)
manicure manicure
mark field
marked market
marskandiser second-hand shop
massage massage
mave stomach
mavepine stomachache
med with
medbragt mad picnic
medicin medicine (drug)
meget much; very
mejeri dairy

mekaniker mechanic

mellem between

mellemmåltid snack

men but

menstruation period (menstrual)

menu menu

mere more

messe fair (event); mass (religious service)

meter meter

metro subway [underground BE]

metrostation subway [underground BE] station

middag dinner; noon

midlertidig temporary

midnat midnight

midten middle

mindesmærke memorial

mindre less

mindst at least

minut minute

miste lose

mobiltelefon cell [mobile BE] phone

mod against; toward

modtageren betaler call collect [reverse the charges BE]

moms sales tax [value-added tax BE]

monument monument

moppe *n* mop

morgen morning

morgenmad breakfast

morgenvækning wake-up call

moské mosque

motel motel

motionscenter gym

motorbåd motorboat

motorcykel motorcycle

motorvej highway [motorway BE]

mund mouth

mundvand mouthwash

mur wall

museum museum

musical musical

musik music

muskel muscle

myggenet mosquito net

mængde quantity

møbel furniture

mødelokale conference room

mødes meet

mønster pattern

mønt coin

møntvaskeri laundromat [launderette BE]

mørk dark

må may (can)

målekrus measuring cup

måleske measuring spoon

måltid meal

måne moon

måned month

måske perhaps

måtte must (have to)

N

narkose anesthetic
nat night
nationalitet nationality
naturlig natural
navn name
ned down
nedenunder below
nederdel skirt
negl nail (body)
neglefil nail file
negleklipper nail clippers
neglesalon nail salon
nej no
nem easy
nerve nerve
nogen any; anyone; someone; some
noget anything; some; something
nogle some
nok enough
nord north
normal *adj* normal
normalt *adv* usually
notesbog notebook
nu now
nummer number
ny new
nyre kidney
nær near
næse nose
næste next

nødhjælpskasse first-aid kit
nødstilfælde emergency
nødudgang emergency exit
nødvendig required
nøgle key
nøglekort key card
nål *n* pin (brooch); needle

O

objektiv lens (camera)
og and
også also; too
omkring around (approximately)
omkørsel detour (traffic)
område region
ondt i halsen sore throat
ondt i ørerne earache
op up
opera opera; opera house
operation operation
oplukker bottle opener
opsparingskonto savings account
optaget busy; occupied
optiker optician
opvarme *v* heat
opvaskemaskine dishwasher
opvaskemiddel detergent
orange orange (color)
ord word
ordbog dictionary
orkester orchestra
oval oval

ovenpå above; upstairs
overfald *n* attack; mugging
overfart crossing (maritime)
overfor opposite
overførsel transfer (money wire)
overskud *n* profit
overskæg moustache
overslag *n* estimate
oversætte translate
overtjener head waiter
ovn stove
oxygenbehandling oxygen treatment

P

pakke package [parcel BE]
papir paper
papirhandel stationery store
papirhåndklæde paper towel
papirslommetørklæde tissue
par pair
paraply umbrella
parfume perfume
park *n* park
parkering parking
parkeringskælder parking garage
parkeringsplads parking lot [car park BE]
parkeringsskive parking disc
parkometer parking meter
pas passport
pasfoto passport photo

paskontrol passport control
passe *v* fit
patient patient
pc computer
pedicure pedicure
pege *v* point
pen pen
penge money
pengeautomat ATM
penicillin penicillin
pensionat guesthouse
pensioneret retired
pensionist senior citizen
per dag per day
per person per person
per time per hour
per uge per week
perle pearl
perron platform (station)
person person
personale staff
personlig personal
petit petite
pibe pipe
pige girl
pille pill; tablet (medical)
pincet tweezers
pinkode PIN
plads seat
pladsreserveringen reservations office
planetarium planetarium

plaster *n* bandage [plaster BE]
plastic plastic
plasticpose plastic bag
plastikfolie plastic wrap
platin platinum
plet stain
plombe filling (tooth)
pløk peg (tent)
politi police
politianmeldelse police report
politistation police station
porcelæn porcelain
portier porter
portion portion
porto postage
post *n* mail [post BE]
postanvisning money order
poste restante general delivery
posthus post office
postkasse mailbox [postbox BE]
postkort postcard
pottemageri pottery
praktiserende læge doctor [general
  practitioner BE]
presse press (iron)
pris price
privat private
procentsats percentage
program program (of events)
proptrækker corkscrew
protese denture
præsentation introduction (social)

præsentere introduce
præventivmiddel contraceptive
prøverum fitting room
pudder powder
pude pillow
pumpe pump
pund pound (British currency, weight)
punktering puncture
pyjamas pajamas
pære light bulb
på on
på landet countryside
pålidelig reliable

R

rabat discount
rabatkort booklet (of tickets)
radio radio
rav amber
reb rope
recept prescription
reception reception
receptionist receptionist
redningsbælte life preserver
redningsbåd life boat
redningvest life jacket
regnemaskine calculator
regnfrakke raincoat
regning check [bill BE] (restaurant)
regnvejr rain
rejse journey; travel; trip
rejsebureau travel agency

rejsecheck traveler's check [cheque BE]

rejsefører guidebook

rejsefører travel guide

rektangulær rectangular

religion religion

ren clean; pure

rensecreme cleansing cream

renseri dry cleaner

rente interest (finance)

reparation *n* repair

reparere *v* fix; mend

reservation reservation

reserveret reserved

rest *n* rest

restaurant restaurant

ret dish (food item)

retsbygning court house

returbillet round-trip [return BE] ticket

returnere return (come back)

reumatisme rheumatism

ribben rib

ridning horseback riding

rigtigt right (correct)

ring ring (jewelry)

ringeklokke bell (electric)

rive i stykker *v* tear

robåd rowboat

rolig calm

romantisk romantic

roomservice room service

rubin ruby

rullegardin blind (window)

rulletrappe escalator

rumtemperatur room temperature

rund round

runde round (golf)

rundt om around (the corner)

rundtur sightseeing tour

rustfrit stål stainless steel

rute route

ryg back

ryge smoke

rygrad spine

rygsæk backpack

rød red

røntgenfotografere X-ray

røre *v* touch

rådhus town hall

S

safir sapphire

saks scissors

sal hall (room)

saldo balance (finance)

salg *n* sale

samme same

sand sand

sandal sandal

sang song

satin satin

sauna sauna

scooter scooter

se *v* look
seddel bill (bank note)
sejlbåd sailboat
sekund second
sele seat belt
sende send
senere later
seng bed
sent late (time)
separeret separated (relationship)
servere serve (meal)
service på værelset room service
serviet napkin
seværdighed point of interest
shampoo shampoo
side side
siden since
sidst last
sige tell
sightseeing sightseeing
sikker *adj* safe
sikkerhedsnål safety pin
silke silk
skaffe provide
skak chess
skakspil chess set
skarp sharp (pain)
skat tax
ske spoon
skib *n* ship
skilt notice (sign)
skive *n* slice

skjorte shirt
sko shoe
skodde shutter (window)
skoforretning shoe store
skole school
Skotland Scotland
skov forest
skovl *n* shovel
skrald garbage [rubbish BE]
skrive write
skrive recept på prescribe
skruetrækker screwdriver
skrædder tailor
skubbe *v* push
skulder shoulder
skulle have (must)
skulptur sculpture
sky cloud
skæg beard
skøjte *v* skate
skøjtebane skating rink
skønhedssalon beauty salon
slags sort (kind)
slagter butcher
slebet glas cut glass
slette *v* clear
slips tie
slipseklemme tie clip
slot palace
sluge swallow
slutning end
smal narrow

smaragd emerald
smerte ache; pain
smerter i brystet chest pain
smerter i ryggen backache
smertestillende middel analgesic; painkiller
sminke *n* make-up
smitsom contagious
smuk beautiful
snackbar snack bar
snart soon
snevejr snow
snitsår *n* cut (wound)
snor string
snorkeludstyr snorkeling equipment
sokke sock
sol sun
solbriller sunglasses
solcreme sun-tan lotion
solforbrænding sunburn
solid sturdy
solstik sunstroke
sort black
souvenir souvenir
souvenirbutik souvenir shop
sove *v* sleep
sovepille sleeping pill
sovepose sleeping bag
sovevogn sleeping car
spa spa
spand bucket; pail
spatel spatula

specialist specialist
specialitet speciality
spejl mirror
spil game
spillehal arcade
spillekort playing card
spise eat
spiseolie oil
spisesalen dining room
spisevogn dining car
spor track (train)
sport sport
sportsforretning sporting goods store
sporvogn tram
springvand fountain
sprog language
spænding voltage
spørgsmål *n* question
stadium stadium
stave *v* spell
stearinlys candle
sted *n* place
stegepande frying pan
stel frame (glasses)
sterlingsølv sterling silver
sti path
stige af get off
stik plug (electric)
stik *n* sting
stikkontakt electrical outlet
stikpille suppository

stille quiet
stilling occupation
stjerne star
stjæle steal
stof cloth; fabric; material
stol chair
stoppet blocked
stor big; large
stor størrelse plus-size
storartet great (excellent)
Storbritannien Great Britain
stormagasin department store
strand beach
strikvarer knitwear
strygejern iron (clothing)
strøm current (ocean)
strømpe stockings
strømpebukser panty hose
studere study
studerende student
studsning trim
stuepige maid
stykke piece; play (theater)
stærk strong
stævnemøde date (appointment)
støjende noisy
størrelse size
støvle boot
støvsuger vacuum cleaner
stå op get up
sulten hungry
supermarked supermarket

sut pacifier [dummy BE] (baby's)
sutteflaske baby bottle
svamp sponge
svar answer
svimmel dizzy
svimmingpool pool
svuppert plunger
svær difficult
svømme v swim
svømmebassin pool
svømning swimming
sweater sweater
sweatshirt sweatshirt
sy sew
syd south
syg ill [BE]
sygdom disease; illness
sygeforsikring health insurance
sygeplejerske nurse
symbol symbol
syn eyesight
synagoge synagogue
synge sing
synshæmmet visually impaired
syntetisk synthetic
system system
sæbe soap
sæde ved midtergangen aisle seat
sælge sell
særlig special
sæson season
sætning sentence

sætte put
sætte sig sit down
sø lake
sød sweet
sølv silver
sølvtøj silverware
så then
sår wound

T

tab loss
tage take
tage imod v accept
tage med bring; to go [take away BE]
tage mål af measure
tage tøjet af undress
taget taken (occupied)
tak thank you
takke thank
tale v speak
tallerken plate
tampon tampon
tand tooth
tandbørste toothbrush
tandlæge dentist
tandpasta toothpaste
tandpine toothache
tarm bowel
taske case (camera)
taske bag (purse)
taxa taxi
taxaholdeplads taxi stand [rank BE]

teater theater
tegnebog wallet
telefon n telephone
telefonbog telephone directory
telefonboks telephone booth
telefonist operator
telefonkort phone card
telefonnummer telephone number
telt tent
teltpløk tent peg
teltstang tent pole
teltunderlag groundsheet
tempel temple
temperatur temperature
tennisbane tennis court
tenniskamp tennis match
tennisketsjer tennis racket
terminal terminal
termometer thermometer
terrasse terrace
teske teaspoon
tid n time
tidligt early
til to
til lykke congratulations
til tiden on time
til venstre left
tilbehør accessory
tillæg n supplement
time hour (time)
tinlegering pewter
tjekke ud v check out

tjener waiter
tobak tobacco
tobakshandler tobacconist
tog train
togkort subway [underground BE] map
toilet restroom [toilet BE]
toiletartikel toiletry
toiletpapir toilet paper
told customs; duty
toldangivelsesformular customs declaration form
toldfri butik duty-free shop
toldfri varer duty-free goods
tolk interpreter
tom empty
tommelfinger thumb
torden thunder
tordenvejr thunderstorm
trafiklys traffic light
transportabel portable
trappe stairs
travlt hurry
trist gloomy
tro think (believe)
tryk pressure
træ tree
trække v pull
trække vejret breathe
trækul charcoal
træt tired

tråd thread
trådløs wireless
T-shirt T-shirt
tube tube
tung heavy
tunge tongue
tur tour
turistkontor tourist office
tynd thin
tyv thief
tyveri robbery
tyveri theft
tæppe blanket
tøj clothing
tøjbutik clothing store
tør dry
tørklæde scarf
tørstig thirsty
tå toe
tåge fog
tårn tower

U

uden without
udenfor outside
udenlandsk foreign
udenrigsfly international flight
udflugt excursion
udfylde fill in (form)
udgang n exit
udgift expense

udkigspost *n* overlook
udlejning rental
udlejningsbil rental car
udsalg sale (bargains)
udsigt view (panorama)
udskrive *v* print (document)
udslet rash
udsolgt out of stock; sold out
udspecificeret regning itemized bill
udstilling exhibition
udstillingsmontre display case
udstyr appliance; equipment
udtale pronunciation
udtryk expression
uge week
uld wool
ulykke accident
under under
underbukser underpants
underkop saucer
underlig strange
underrette notify
underskrift signature
underskrive sign
undersøgelse check-up (medical)
undertrøje undershirt
undervisning lesson
undskylde *v* excuse
ung young
universitet university
ur clock; watch

USA United States
uskyldig innocent

V

vaccinere vaccinate
valuta currency
vand water
vandfald waterfall
vandhane faucet
vandrehjem youth hostel
vandski waterski
vandtæt waterproof
vare article (merchandise)
varm hot; warm (temperature)
varme heat [heating BE]
vaske i hånden hand washable
vaske *v* wash
vaskemaskine washing machine
vaskeri laundry service
vaskerum laundry facilities
vaskesuger plunger
vasketøj laundry
ved at
ved siden af next to
vedhæng pendant
vegetar vegetarian
vej road; way
vejangivelse direction
vejkort road map
vejkryds crossroads; intersection
vejr weather

vejrudsigt weather forecast
vejskilt road sign
vekselkontor currency exchange office
vekselkurs exchange rate
veksle *v* exchange (money)
ven friend
vending phrase
vene vein
vente *v* expect; wait
venteværelse waiting room
ventilator fan
vest west
v-hals v-neck
vi we
vide know
videokamera video camera
vigtig important
vil gerne like
ville have want
vind wind
vindue window
vinduessæde window seat
vinhandel liquor store [off-licence BE]
vinliste wine list
violet purple
virke *v* work
virkelig hyggelig wonderful
virker ikke out of order
vis certain
vise vej til *v* direct (someone)
visitkort business card

viskelæder eraser
voldtægt *n* rape
volleyballkamp volleyball game
væddeløb race
væddeløbsbane race track
væk away
vække wake
vækkeur alarm clock
vælg choice
vær venlig please
værdi value
være be
værelse room (hotel)
værelsesbestillig hotel reservation
værelsesnummer room number
værktøj tool
værre worse
væske fluid
vådservietter baby wipes

W

Wales Wales
weekend weekend
windsurfer windsurfer

Z

zoologisk have zoo

Æ

ædelsten gem
ægte genuine; real
ændre *v* alter

ærme sleeve
æske box

øje eye
øjeblik moment
øjendråber eye drops
øjenskygge eye shadow
økonomiklasse economy class
øm sore (painful)

ønske *v* wish
øre ear
øredråber ear drops
ørenring earring
øst east

Å

åben open
åbne *v* open
år year